Winning Workouts For Competitive Cheerleaders

Thanks for your love and encouragment.

Love Alton

Disclaimer

This Training Manual is not meant to diagnose or treat any medical condition. It is designed as a resource for individuals wishing to follow strength and conditioning program for cheerleading. Individuals with any pre-existing medical conditions should check with their doctor before commencing any program of physical activity. I cannot be held responsible for any injury resulting from the use of this Training Manual or any of the information contain herein. If you are unsure about its suitability for you, always check with a medical professional first.

Winning Workouts for Competitive Cheerleaders

Fly Higher, Stunt Bigger and Reduce Injuries in 15 Minutes

By Alton Skinner

Title ID: 3798614
ISBN-13: 978-1470119133

Contents

Introduction

Introduction

Competitive cheerleading is fast becoming one of the most popular and widely performed sports in the world. The number of athletes and teams increase daily across the United States, Canada, Europe, South America and Asia. It is enjoyed by athletes from very young children through college age athletes and beyond. The sport places incredible physical demands on those who participate in it. It is a multidirectional explosive, stop start, complex and graceful sport. In recent years not only have athletes become stronger and more powerful, but the choreography has become increasing more tumbling and strength based. Competitive cheerleading fuses together the elements of athletic ability, skill, drama and competitiveness that makes it not only fun to do but nearly irresistible to watch.

Consider in an average two and a half minute program there are between 3 and 6 tumbling passes, a similar number of lifts, 20 to 40 seconds of dance combined with the all out sprints required to get into proper positions for stunts and tumbling passes. Then add the hours of training required to perfect the above routine over the course of the longest season of any sport high school or college sport. This sport places extreme demands on an athlete's strength and conditioning.

The sport is incredibly athletic, full of power but also artistic and graceful. There are few things more exciting or inspiring than watching a well choreographed program, executed flawlessly. The athletes demonstrate speed, agility quickness, powerful tumbling, dynamic flexibility, athletic prowess and precision team work all under the extreme pressure of competition.

The attributes of speed, strength, flexibility and stamina make the difference between winning and losing at whatever level an athlete or team competes. In the past, the attributes required to perform these elaborate programs were neglected in most practices. Today however, progressive coaches, athletes and choreographers believe training these attributes are essential for success in competitive cheer leading.

This program is the first cheer specific training program to focus on the introduction of a progressive athlete development model to the sport of competitive cheer leading for middle school, high school and all star athletes. This is the first in a series of programs. This program has numerous benefits like reducing injuries, improving hand and foot strength/coordination and developing strength and core control. It is full of variety and fun challenges for all athletes.

It is designed to be progressive teaching based on complex sport science concepts but practical to use and easy to understand. This program will help with long term athletic development and multi-skilled training. The desired results are powerful, flexible, explosive athletic skills specific for the sport of cheer leading.

This program is designed to be adapted to meet the needs of all ages, and can be used for both individual and squad training. This program will add new tools and skills for coaches, athletes and parents to use to develop their young athletes potential. This book will help coaches, parents, and players to understand the how and why of this program. It will provide clear precise examples of how to put sports theory onto the competition floor.

To compete at a high level requires athletes to have world class strength, flexibility, endurance and mental toughness. Competition today demands higher jumps, kicks, flips, lifts and more elaborate tumbling from each athlete integrated into a two and half minute performance that must be executed with military precision in order to place, let alone win in competition. This creates a dilemma for athletes and coaches, how to balance the time required perfecting the routine, improving skills, training for improved performance and injury prevention. Project All Star is an attempt to solve this problem. In an era where innovation equals wins it is a must to add strength and conditioning element to your program.

This program is about how to turn the all important first and last fifteen minutes of practice into the minutes when you get the edge that will separate your team from the rest. In my research I discovered that most cheer teams can realistically and consistently include only about 15 minutes of conditioning in a competition practice session. I also discovered that the current approach is often unstructured and not based on the newest research into performance enhancement.

I have sought to design a series of movements that will maximize improvement in the fifteen minute window at practice. My hope is that the programs prove to be so beneficial coaches and athletes will expand the time they commit to improving performance through strength and conditioning.

Winning Workouts for Competitive Cheerleaders is a collection of training drills, protocols and programs designed to maximize performance and reduce injuries for your athletes in a time efficient manner.

This program will attempt to achieve our objectives:

1) Reduce the frequency and severity of injuries during skill training and performances.
2) Improve the overall athletic ability of every member of the team
3) Develop athletes with the ability to perform progressively more challenging choreography to create a competitive advantage.
4) Teach a basic understanding of the modern fundamentals of training

The purpose of this program is to provide a versatile training template to allow a single athlete or large team of athletes to be trained quickly, safely, effectively and easily. I wanted to design a program that offered a large number of workouts but required the mastery of only a small number of exercises. I wanted to design a program that could be implemented with a lost cost of entry. I wanted design a program that could teach training fundamentals and was scalable over the athletes training lifetime. I wanted to design a program easy enough to follow that an athlete, parent or coach could utilize it without have a degree in exercise science or some sort of training certification and still produce profound results. I wanted to design a program that would allow cheer and dance athletes to train to improve performance and reduce injuries in a time efficient manner so that they could focus on skill training to perfect their programs.

This program is divided into four sections.

A dynamic warm-up specific designed for cheer leaders to immediately improve their performance.

A strength training exercise section that explains the how, why, when and what type of exercise to perform.

A program design section to show you how to put together your own program.

A sample training program section that puts together dozens of sample training programs to follow or use as a place to generate programs of your own.

Please stay in touch I'd like to know how close I came to my goals I set with this program. Feedback is the breakfast of champions, I know this program is far from exhaustive but I wanted it to be useable. I want it to be an entry point into the world of strength and conditioning and the remarkable benefits it offers for the sport of competitive cheer leading. I encourage questions and comments and I will use them to improve each future version of this manual.

Website: http://www.altonskinner.com
Twitter: altonskinner
LinkedIn: http://www.linkedin.com/pub/alton-skinner/3a/714/503
Facebook: AltonSkinner
Blog: http://winningworkoutsforcompetitivecheerleaders.wordpress.com
Google+profile: https://plus.google.com/u/0/116082159178277141343/posts

Why Use This Program?

One of the greatest benefit of following this plan it the powerful injury prevention and rehabilitating effects this type of training offers your athletes. Competitive cheerleaders are at risk for a number of injuries, ranging from bumps, bruises, broken bones, sprains and strains. This program will address this injury risk in a number of ways.

Below are some injury statistics collected from the Journal of Athletic Training.

Most common cheerleading injuries:

1. *Ankle sprain or strain 15%*
2. *Neck sprain or strain 7%*
3. *Lower back strain or sprain 5 %*
4. *Knee strain or sprain 5%*
5. *Wrist strain or sprain 4%*

Top Five body parts injured

1. *Ankle 16%*
2. *Knee 9%*
3. *Neck 9%*
4. *Lower back 7%*
5. *Head 7%*

Most injuries occur during practice 83% and 38% of these injuries occur 61 to 90 minutes into the practice.
52% of injuries occur during a stunt, 28% of injuries occur during tumbling.
Bases are more likely to be injured than fliers 24% compared to 14% from falls.
15% of injuries occurred while failing to complete a stunt. Another 15% occurred during tumbling.
In All Star cheer leading most injuries occur during tumbling. The second most common source of injury is collision with another cheerleader.

So how can we as coaches reduce these injuries through a fitness approach?

The first method I propose to decrease injury and increase power output is by using an innovative dynamic mobility and warm-up series prior to practice, training, and/or performance. By replacing traditional static stretches and a quick run, with an integrated mobility progression your athletes will produce more power immediately according to numerous studies. Hopefully, everyone realizes by now that static stretching can reduce strength. It can also decrease power output by as much as 17% for up to 90 minutes. By that time, the competition or training session is over!

The National Academy of Sports Medicine's position on static stretching is that when done prior to an exercise session, static stretching may in fact decrease the athlete's ability to generate power during the activity. For example a cheerleader or dancer's elevation may actually be reduced when static stretching is done before technique class, rehearsal or performance. It is suggested rather that a better warm up regimen might be to engage in self myofascial release (foam rolling) followed by dynamic stretching and perhaps a light cardiovascular warm up with movement rehearsal.

The second method I propose is to add a structured, developmental strength and conditioning program.

This program will strengthen every muscle, tendon and ligament from head to toe. Also, many athletes have low back pain; this program will help strengthen hips, glutes, and abs and back muscles in a manner that will minimize the chance of injury during lifting, tumbling, and stunting. Whether for a flyer or base this plan will help improve performance and reduce the chance of injuries.

This program will improve the mobility, stability and strength of the shoulder complex, just the thing to keep this often injured area healthy.

The ballistic nature of this training will strengthen joints, creating a strong agile body that can withstand the demanding toll that a modern cheerleader takes on the ankles, wrist, neck, knees and back.

The acceleration and deceleration of required for the drills in this program will strengthen tendons and ligaments while increasing strength and mobility in order to reduce the chance of injury. This type of training will prepare an athlete's body to absorb force more efficiently. This means that as a base they can handle the loading and unloading of your flyers better. Your flyers will be able to better handle being tossed, falling and caught. Also the athletes will better tolerate the forces generated during tumbling.

This plan will develop a more athletic cheerleadr. Following these training programs will develop the serious stamina required for today's high energy performances without spending hours doing boring and repetitive cardiovascular training. These workouts combine cardio and strength training. Also, this program will help develop the strength and stamina required to maximize performance during long practice sessions leading up to competition.

Here is what research reveals about the value of supplemental training for dance and cheer.

Many of the skills required in dance and cheer are also used in sports like figure skating and gymnastics (McQueen, 1986). Certain sport training techniques, therefore, can be useful to dancers (McQueen, 1986). Fahey (2000) noted that, "Jumping exercises and plyometrics enhance performance in strength-speed sports because they increase leg power and train the nervous system to activate large muscle groups when you move" (p. 76). Hutchinson and colleagues' study of elite gymnasts suggested that leap training utilizing a swimming pool as well as Pilates safely enhanced leaping ability (Hutchinson, Tremain, Christiansen, & Beitzel, 1998). ***In the study, after one month of training, gymnasts improved their*** **explosive power by 220%, their ground reaction time by 50%, and the height of their leaps by 16.2%.**

These workouts consist of whole body movements just like our sport. Your team will improve their muscle tone, body composition and strength. They will also strengthen tendons and ligaments, making joints tougher and less susceptible to injury. Your athletes will train movements, not muscles to improve whole body athleticism. They will develop strength as it relates to the mobility required in competitive cheerleading while improving stamina and strength at the same time.

They will improve their power to weight ratio. These routines require a lot of energy to perform while developing lean muscle. This will help develop a leaner and stronger athlete. These programs will create a lean, athletic non bulky body in a short period of time. This will allow your time to fly higher, tumble faster and perform more difficult stunts.

The third method I propose in this program is to use unstable objects in the strength and conditioning program. By using sandbags, kettlebells, and other pieces of equipment your athletes will train their muscles in a manner that shows up in a performance. Using odd, unstable loads is a better match for the requirements of your sport. Lifting other athletes, stunting and tumbling all involve handling shifting weight and centers of gravity. By training with these programs your teams will be able to perform better, faster and safer.

What does current research reveal for modern cheerleaders?

Lifting another person off the ground occurs rapidly, and therefore supplemental power training may be highly useful- Olympic exercises such as power cleans, the snatch, and the clean and jerk can have specificity for any dancers who routinely execute lifts, and can be modified to provide greater specificity for dance movement. Supplemental plyometric training may also be of benefit for dancers. Dancers typically train for jumps by practicing jumps; at the barre the dancer first learns to plie-releve rapidly, before replacing the releve with a auté, or jump. This is essentially plyometric training and while dancers may be highly successful jumpers through dance training alone, it is possible that performance may be enhanced through application of supplemental strength and power training for the jumping muscles, as increases in maximal strength and power may increase the athlete's ability to execute and recover from bouts of plyometric training, i.e. the repeated jumps and leaps in dance[4].

Your athletes will develop the serious stamina that matches the demands of your routines and practice sessions. You will develop a group with an athletic posture that is as functional as it is visually pleasing on the floor. This program is great for competitive cheerleaders, it develops strength at the extremes range of motions required to excel in modern cheer. This program will stabilize joints, improve flexibility and enhance mobility. This means all your stunts will be rock solid from the base to the flyer.

By improving overall conditioning, cheerleaders and teams following this program will be capable of executing more and more challenging choreography. This program will help develop explosive power for jumps, tumbling and lifting. Also, cheerleaders will develop strength endurance. It's easy to be powerful once, but can your athletes do it over and over again perfectly? Competitive cheerleaders must be strong, powerful and perfect over repeated efforts during practice and performance. This plan will give your athletes the ability to train up to your standards.

Who Can Use This Program?

The drills in this program are easy to learn. The movements are simple and you can start using them right away. ***This program is designed to be safe for ages 11 and up***. You don't have to worry about which exercise require which weight. You don't have to worry about what days to do cardio or strength training. You don't need to worry about upper body drills and lower body drills. It's all in one.

This program will teach athletes basic fundamentals of training for modern cheerleading. The training methods use classic, basic, timeless exercises that can and should be used throughout an athlete's life. What is unique is the versatility offered in the pairing, grouping, rest periods, length and a number of other attributes to create numerous programs without learning numerous exercises.

As athletes perform these drills your team will develop strength without the monotony of isolated exercises. These workouts will help develop the flexibility that meets the unique need of competitive cheerleading without long sessions. These training programs are versatile. Athletes will improve strength to weight ratio, build muscle, and enhance performance with a few simple drills. Following this program is a time efficient method to developing a strong, powerful, and flexible and injury resistance team.

When to Use This Program Work?

These workouts use small, compact and portable devices. That means your athletes can train anywhere, the gym, home, or outside. This will allow athletes to train consistently without investing lots of time just getting to the training center. These workouts are great for today's busy athlete. This program will use multiple methods to boost performance.

These drills can be assigned to individuals to be performed at home or performed at the end of practice.

My preferred format:

1. 5-15 minute dynamic warm-up
2. General tumbling warm-up, motions, and jumps
3. Basic lifts and stunts. Progressing from unloaded to loaded.
4. Skill development
5. 15 to 20 minute strength and conditioning
6. Specific flexibility development
7. Review session, set goals for next practice, assign home training, and answer athlete's questions

How Often Do I Use This Program?

I recommend my athletes perform two strength sessions per week either at end of practice and/or at home during the season. During the off season I like to train 3 to 4 days depending on an athlete's age and goals.

What Methods Does This Program Use?

The first method will be the use of complexes. In this method you combine two or more exercises performed back to back using the same resistance. For example you may group together a bent over row, shoulder press, and a squat. Athletes would do all the required repetitions of the bent over row, then move directly to the shoulder press, complete the required number and then move directly into the squat, all without ever putting down the weight. Usually athletes perform 5 to 10 repetitions of each drill. You then repeat this entire collection for the required number of sets.

Another method you will use is density training. Density training is an excellent match for the requirements of today's athletes. Density training is about performing more work in a given time period. It works like this, you pick five exercises each loaded with a weight you can perform about 10 to 12 repetitions. Athletes then perform 8 reps of each drill until you perform all of them; they continue to move through the circuit until the time is up. For example, how many times can they complete a series of bent over rows, lunges, shoulder press, zercher squats and kettle bell swings in 15 minutes?

Another way to use the same principle is to see how quickly they can perform 5 rounds of 8 reps in each of the bent over row, lunge, shoulder press, zercher squats and kettle bell swings.

One method helps develop strength endurance the other helps develop speed strength, both are key to maximizing your performance. The goal is to develop fitter athletes that can either perform your planned choreography more easily resulting in fewer errors or better able to handle more difficult stunts. You may also use this method to develop athletes that are fit and strong enough to include more elements in the 2:30 seconds allowed in competition.

This program also uses a timed method of intervals with varying ratios of work to rest periods. An example would be 30 seconds of squats followed by 30 seconds of rest for 8 rounds. The goal here is to achieve the maximum number of repetitions during the work interval.

Timing Options for Density Training

This program also uses a timed method of intervals with varying ratios of work to rest periods. An example would be 30 seconds of squats followed by 30 seconds of rest for 8 rounds. The goal here is to achieve the maximum number of repetitions during the work interval.

What follows are some example workouts:

Option One. Defined Time. This options works as follows, decide on a set time period, determine the number of exercises to be used, and see how many sets of the exercises you can complete in the time period.

I use 10, 15 or 20 minute blocks of depending on how practice is going. I pick 3 to 5 exercises and see how many times my athlete can complete the circuit. Record the weight, the total sets, post the results and try to beat the total sets in the next session.

For Example:

Total Time 15 minutes		Weight	Total Sets:
Sandbag Shouldering	10Reps		
Two Hand Kettlebell Swing	10 Reps		
Sand Bag Bent Over Rows	10 Reps		
Kettlebell Clean Right Hand	10 Reps		
Kettlebell Clean Left Hand	10 Reps		

Option Two. Defined Sets. With this options you set the goal of completing a set series of exercises with sets weight and repetitions and see how quickly you can complete the required number of circuits.

For example, take the exact exercise from above and set the session up in the following manner.

Total Time: As Fast as Possible Three Circuits		Weight	Complete
Sandbag Shouldering	10Reps		
Two Hand Kettlebell Swing	10 Reps		
Sand Bag Bent Over Rows	10 Reps		
Kettlebell Clean Right Hand	10 Reps		
Kettlebell Clean Left Hand	10 Reps		

I have had good luck with pairing these sessions on alternate practice days. This has several advantages from a coaching stand point. First, it saves times, one set of drills provides two or more training sessions, allowing coaches to focus on other areas. Second, this training method reinforces a competitive spirit in the athletes. These type of workouts automatically create a situation where an athlete has a clearly defined target they must reach and surpass. The athlete is competing against themselves which over time develops a self motivated desire to achieve personal excellence.

Option Three. Set work to Rest Intervals. With this option, you define a time for each work set, followed by a defined rest period. The goal is to add more reps during the work period as you get fitter and stronger. There are numerous versions of this option. 10-15-20 minutes work well for this option

3030 sets. A very popular interval is a 1:1 work to rest ratio of 30 seconds on 30 seconds off. I'll use the same workouts above to illustrates this point

Total Time: 15 minutes	30:30 work /rest	Reps
Sandbag Shouldering		
Two Hand Kettlebell Swing		

Sand Bag Bent Over Rows

Kettlebell Clean Right Hand

Kettlebell Clean Left Hand

This will result in three sets of each exercise being performed. This allows the athlete to compete within each series, each round, each workout and each time they attempt this workout again. In addition to fostering a competitive spirit, this method develops athletes that can perform more work in a defined time period. This will develop the fitness require to execute all out, every time during a 2:30 minute routine. 10-15-20 minute session work great for competitive cheerleaders.

Option Four: Negative Rest to Work Intervals. This is a very challenging option. With this option your athletes use a 2:1 work to rest interval. This method is designed to improve the athlete's recovery and work capacity. For the sport of cheerleading I use a 40sec to 20sec ratio most often. This means an athlete performs a drill for 40 seconds records the reps, rest 20 seconds before moving to the next drill. Each set is about a minute long, 40 second of work along with 20 seconds of rest. The goal is either to perform more reps in the same time next workout or the same reps with a heavier weight the next session.

Using our same sample workout, here's how this option works

Total Time: 15 minutes   40:20sec work /rest   Reps

Sandbag Shouldering

Two Hand Kettlebell Swing

Sand Bag Bent Over Rows

Kettlebell Clean Right Hand

Kettlebell Clean Left Hand

This will result in three sets of each exercise being performed.

Again this allows the athlete to compete within each series, each round, each workout and each time they attempt this workout again. This will develop the fitness require to execute all out, every time during a 2:30 minute routine. 10-15-20 minute session work great for competitive cheerleaders.

Option Five: Positive Work to Rest Intervals. With this option, the athlete rest longer than the work period. A common period is 1:3 work to rest ratio. For cheerleading, I like to use 30 seconds on to 90 seconds off. This gives the athlete a nice, neat 2 minute set which makes it easier to setup a workout circuit. This option allows for more work to be performed during the work period. This means either a heavier load or more reps since the athlete has a longer period to recover.

Using our same sample workout, here's how this option works

Total Time: 20 minutes	30:90 sec work /rest	Reps
Sandbag Shouldering		
Two Hand Kettlebell Swing		
Sand Bag Bent Over Rows		
Kettlebell Clean Right Hand		
Kettlebell Clean Left Hand		

This results in two complete rotations. Again the goal is to either increase the reps or weight used the next time this workout is performed.

Option Six: Set Number of Repetitions. With this option, the athlete use a set number or repetitions instead of a set work period, with the goal of decrease the time it takes to complete all the required repetitions. For cheerleaders, I recommend beginning with 10 and progressing until reaching the goal of 20 reps of a drill.

Sample Progression

Total Time: As Fast as Possible	Session			
	One	Two	Three	Four
Sandbag Shouldering	10	12	15	20
Two Hand Kettlebell Swing	10	12	15	20
Sand Bag Bent Over Rows	10	12	15	20
Kettlebell Clean Right Hand	10	12	15	20
Kettlebell Clean Left Hand	10	12	15	20

As you can see density training is a varied, simple, effective and versatile method to improve your athlete's performance quickly.

What follows are some example workouts:

Warm-up Exercises Descriptions and Demonstrations

Warm-up Exercises Descriptions and Demonstrations

A quality conditioning program for cheerleading includes strength, flexibility, and endurance training. If any component of a competitive cheerleading training program is neglected, these athletes are unlikely to achieve their full potential and are more susceptible to injury while training and performing. Competitive cheerleading demands proper warm-up and flexibility training for all areas of the body. Injuries to the upper and lower extremities as wells as the trunk have been reported in elite and recreational athletes.

The warm-up plays an important part in the conditioning program. The purpose of the warm-up is to prepare the body tissues to optimally respond to the exercises and stretches used during the workout and to prevent injury. Athletes often use two types of warm-up. A passive warm-up involves applying an external heat to the body. Examples of passive warm-ups include applying moist heat packs, heating pads, or a warm whirlpool before exercise. These techniques increase tissue temperature, but are not always practical. A second type of warm-up is the active warm-up and involves low intensity exercise which elevates tissue temperature, increases heart rate, and actively prepares the athlete for practice, performance or exercise. In chart below is a sample dynamic warm up that will prepare an athlete for optimum performance.

Working until you experience a light sweat indicates the proper duration and intensity of a warm-up. Using the recommend activities, you can often achieve this in three to five minutes. Additional benefits of a proper warm-up are improved muscle elasticity and a reduced risk of muscle and tendon injury.

By replacing traditional static stretches and a quick run, with an integrated mobility progression your athletes will produce more power immediately according to numerous studies. Hopefully, everyone realizes by now that static stretching can reduce strength. **It can also decrease power output by as much as 17% for up to 90 minutes. By that time, the competition or training session is over!**

The National Academy of Sports Medicine's position on static stretching is that when done prior to an exercise session, static stretching may in fact decrease the athlete's ability to generate power during the activity. For example a cheerleader or dancer's elevation may actually be reduced when static stretching is done before technique class, rehearsal or performance. It is suggested rather that a better warm up regimen might be to engage in self myofascial release (foam rolling) followed by dynamic stretching and perhaps a light cardiovascular warm up with movement rehearsal.

On the following pages are charts of warm-up drills and instructions on how to perform them for maximum benefit.

Drill	Reps		
Jumping Jacks	15		
Seal Jumps with leg switches	15		
Pogo Jumps	20		
Full Body Circles(Clockwise)	10		
Full Body Circles(Counter Clockwise)	10		
Arm Circles Forward	10		
Arm Circles Backward	10		
Elbow Circles Clockwise	10		
Elbow Circles Counter Clockwise	10		
Wrist Circles	20		
Shoulder Twist	10		
Toe Touches to overhead reach	3		
Body Weight Squats	10		
Stand To Squat	3		
Pushup Pulses			
4 point stance	10		
On knees	10		

Full plank	10		
One arm pulses	10		
Child pose to Cobra	5		
Striders/Runner Pose Flow	Alternate sides 4 per side		
Striders/Runner Pose Flow with twist	Alternate sides 4 per side		
Hamstring to Hip Flexor Stretch	4 Per side		
Band Pull apart	20		
Band pull apart with dislocation	20		
Backward Roll into Plough back into straddle	6		
Backward Roll into Plough back into hamstring stretch	6		
Backward Roll into Plough back into Glute Stretch	4 per side alternate legs		
Close grip full pushups quickly	10		
Deep Squat to forward lunge	3 per legs alternate		
Cossacks squats/lunge	5 per side		
Standing Glute Stretch	3 per side alternate legs		
Cradle Walks	3 per legs alternate		

Warm-Up Drill Descriptions

Jumping Jacks

Step 1

Stand with your arms at your sides. Be sure your feet are straight and close together.

Step 2

Bend your knees. Jump up while spreading your arms and legs at the same time.

Step 3

Lift your arms to your ears and open your feet to a little wider than shoulder width. This should all be one smooth motion.

Step 4

Clap or touch your hands above your head. As you return from jumping up bring your arms back down to your sides and at the same time bring your feet back together.

Step 5

Repeat for the required number of repetitions

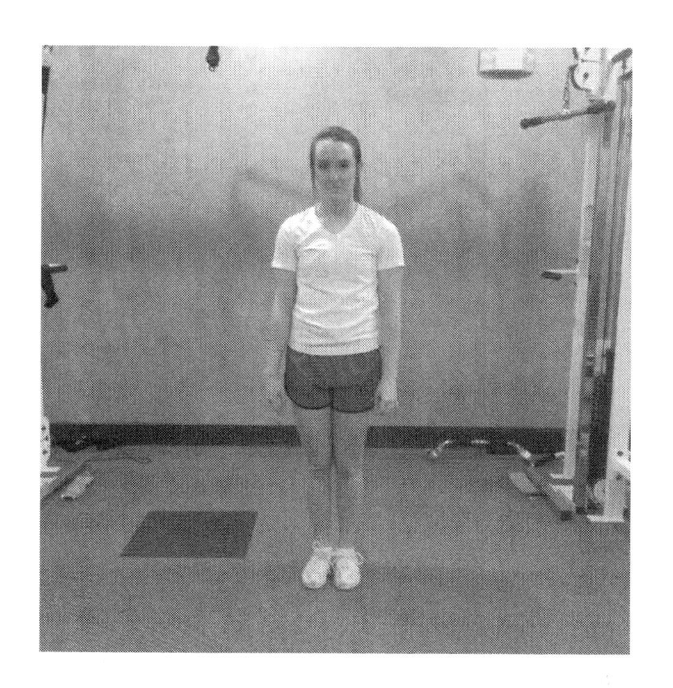

Jumping Jack Start

Jumping Jack Finish

Seal Jumps with Leg Switches

Step 1

Stand with your arms at your sides. Be sure your feet are straight and close together.

Step 2

Bend your knees. Jump up while spreading your arms and legs at the same time.

Step 3

Lift your arms to your shoulder height and open your feet to a little wider than shoulder width. This should all be one smooth motion.

Step 4

With arms extended, cross your right arm over your left arm at chest height while at the same time crossing your right leg in front of your left leg.

Step 5

Jump up while spreading your arms and legs at the same time. Cross your left arm over your right arm while at the same time crossing your left leg in front of your right leg.

Step 6

Continue switching sides in a smooth steady cadence. Repeat for the required number of repetitions.

Seal Jump Start

Step 2

Seal Jump Step 3

Seal Jump Step 4

Low Pogo Jumps

Step 1

Stand with your arms at your sides. Be sure your feet are straight and close together

Step 2 Jump about 1 to 2 inches off the ground.

Step 3

This jump should come just by springing off your ankles.

Step 4

While in the air pull your toes up. Make sure your heels never touch the ground.

Step 5

Keep your body rigid and aligned straight up and down.

Step 6

Make sure you spend as little time on the ground as possible. These are short quick jumps performed rapidly.

Step 7

Repeat for the required number of repetitions.

Pogo Jumps Start

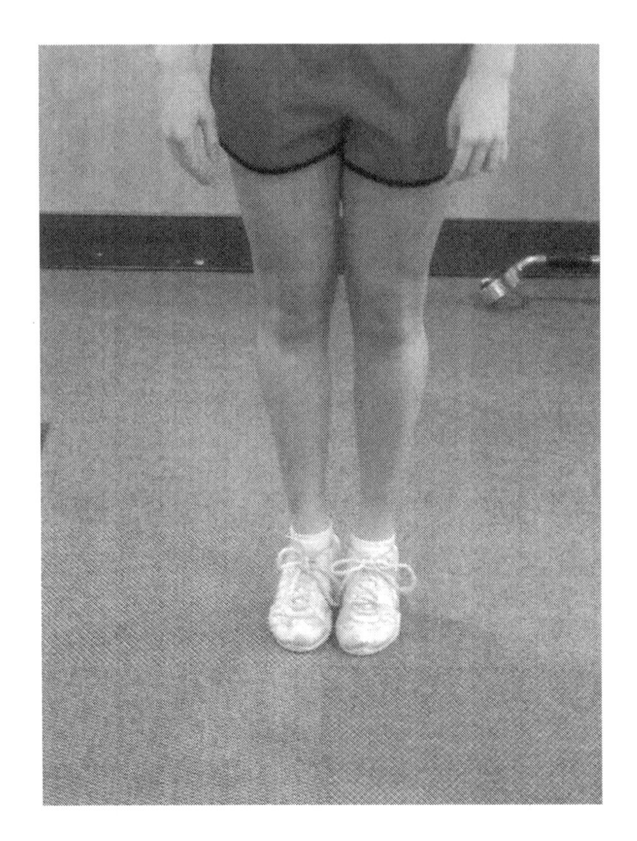

Pogo Jump Action

Full Body Circles

Step 1

Stand with feet slightly wider than shoulder width with your arms clasped at shoulder height.

Step 2

Soften your knees by bending them slightly.

Step 3

Bend forward and draw a large clockwise circle by bending forward at the waist, rotating slowly upward, leaning slightly back, and dropping slowly down to a forward hinge.

Step 4

Repeat for the required number of repetitions in a clockwise direction followed by the required number of repetitions in a counterclockwise direction.

Full Body Circle Step 1

Full Body Circle Step 2

Full Body Circle Step 3

Full Body Circle Step 4

Arm Circles (Forward and Back)

Step 1

Stand with feet slightly wider than shoulder width with your arms clasped at shoulder height.

Step 2

Soften your knees by bending them slightly.

Step 3

Extend your right arm overhead.

Step 4

Slowly rotate your arm backward. Complete one full rotation.

Step 5

Perform the required number of repetitions.

Step 6 Repeat for your left arm.

Step 7

Extend your right arm overhead

Step 8

Rotate your arm forward. Complete one full rotation.

Step 9

Perform the required number of repetitions.

Step 10

Repeat for your left arm.

Step 11

Perform the required number of repetitions.

Arm Circles Forward

Arm Circles Backward

Wrist Circles

Step 1

Stand with feet slightly wider than shoulder width with your arms clasped at shoulder height.

Step 2

Slowly rotate your wrist in a clockwise direction.

Step 3

This is a slow and deliberate motion, designed to take your wrist through a full range of motion.

Step 4

Perform the required number of repetitions.

Step 5

Slowly rotate your wrist in a counter clockwise direction.

Step 6

Perform the required number of repetitions.

Wrist Circles Start

Wrist Circles Step 2

Wrist Circles Step 3

Elbow Circles

Step 1

Stand with feet shoulder width apart. Arms extend at your sides

Step 2

Slowly draw circles by rotating from your elbows.

Step 3

Draw small then larger and larger circles

Step 4

Perform in clockwise and counterclockwise directions

Step 5

Perform for the required number of repetitions.

Elbow Circles Start

Elbow Circles Finish

Shoulder Twist

Step 1

Stand upright and extend both arms straight out to sides.

Step 2

Rotate one "upper arm" forward and down while rotating the opposite "upper arm" backward and down

Step 3

Repeat in opposite directions.

Step 4

Perform for the required number of repetitions.

Shoulder Twist Start

Shoulder Twist Finish

Toe Touch to Overhead Reach

Step 1

Stand with your feet 12 to 16 inches apart.

Step 2

Lift your kneecaps by flexing your thigh muscles.

Step 3

As you exhale, bend at the waist, keeping your legs straight.

Step 4

Keep your weight toward the front of your feet to avoid leaning backwards.

Step 5

Relax your neck, allowing the crown of your head to stretch toward the ground.

Step 6

Return to standing as you extended both arms overhead.

Step 7

Repeat for the required repetitions.

Start

Toe Touch To Overhead Reach 2

Body Weight Squats

Step 1

Stand with feet about shoulder width apart.

Step 2

Squat down with your butt back, your weight on your heels and your lower back in a neutral position.

Step 3

Use your legs to drive upward explosively.

Step 4

Push your hips back, keep your back straight, chest up and get your butt down below your knees. Keep your weight mostly on your heels. Once your reach the bottom of the movement, squeeze your gluts and push off of your heels to get into the standing position.

Step 5

Repeat for the required number of repetitions.

Squat

Stand to Squat

Step 1

Stand with your feet 12 to 16 inches apart.

Step 2

Lift your kneecaps by flexing your thigh muscles.

Step 3

As you exhale, bend at the waist, keeping your legs straight.

Step 4

Keep your weight toward the front of your feet to avoid leaning backwards.

Step 5

Relax your neck, allowing the crown of your head to stretch toward the ground.

Step 6

Place your hands on top of your feet.

Step 7

While keeping your hands on your feet, squat down as low as possible.

Step 8

While keeping your hands on top of your feet, straighten your legs as much as possible.

Step 9

Return to your low squat position.

Step 10

Repeat for the required number of repetitions.

Squat to Stand 1

Squat to Stand 2

Four Point Shoulder Pulses

Step 1

Start on your hands and knees. Position your hands directly beneath your shoulders and your knees directly beneath the hips. Have your fingers fully spread with the middle fingers pointing straight ahead. Make your back horizontal and flat. Look at the floor. This is your "neutral" positioning. When your pelvis is in neutral, your spine will be at full extension, with both the front and back sides equally long.

Step 2

Sink down through your shoulders.

Step 3

Retract your shoulders back. This should be a series of short pulses.

Step 4

Repeat for the required number of repetitions.

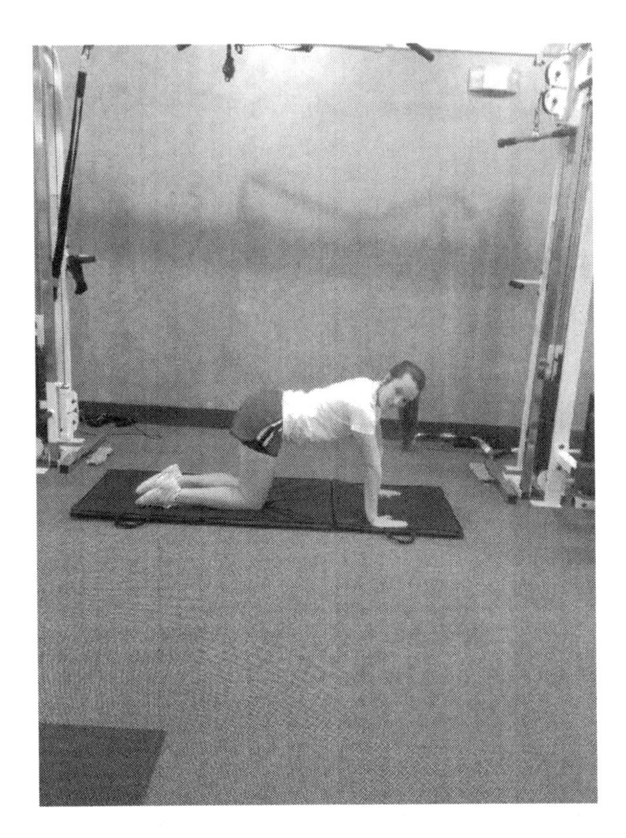

Four Point Shoulder Pulse

Four Point Shoulder Pulses from Knees.

Step 1

Start on your hands and knees. Position your hands directly beneath your shoulders and your knees directly beneath the hips. Have your fingers fully spread with the middle fingers pointing straight ahead. Make your back horizontal and flat. Look at the floor. This is your "neutral" positioning. When your pelvis is in neutral, your spine will be at full extension, with both the front and back sides equally long.

Step 2

Drop your hips until your body forms a 45 degree angle to the floor.

Step 3

Sink down through your shoulders.

Step 4

Retract your shoulders back. This should be a series of short pulses.

Step 5

Repeat for the required number of repetitions.

Shoulder Pulse From Knees

Four Point Shoulder Pulses from Plank Positions

Step 1

Start on your hands and knees. Position your hands directly beneath your shoulders and your knees directly beneath the hips. Have your fingers fully spread with the middle fingers pointing straight ahead. Make your back horizontal and flat. Look at the floor. This is your "neutral" positioning. When your pelvis is in neutral, your spine will be at full extension, with both the front and back sides equally long.

Step 2

Drop your hips and extend your legs until your body is parallel to the floor.

Step 3

Sink down through your shoulders.

Step 4

Retract your shoulders back. This should be a series of short pulses.

Step 5

Repeat for the required number of repetitions.

Pulse From Plank

One Arm Shoulder Pulses from Plank Positions

Step 1

Start on your hands and knees. Position your hands directly beneath your shoulders and your knees directly beneath the hips. Have your fingers fully spread with the middle fingers pointing straight ahead. Make your back horizontal and flat. Look at the floor. This is your "neutral" positioning. When your pelvis is in neutral, your spine will be at full extension, with both the front and back sides equally long.

Step 2

Drop your hips and extend your legs until your body is parallel to the floor.

Step 3

Sink down through your shoulders of your right arm.

Step 4

Retract your shoulders back.

Step 5

Sink down through your shoulders of your left arm.

Step 6

Retract your shoulders back.

This should be a series of short alternating pulses.

Step 7

Repeat for the required number of repetitions.

One Shoulder Pulse From Plank

Close Grip Pushups: Quickly As Possible.

Step 1

Assume a plank position. Place your hands right under your shoulders with your fingers pointing forward. This is called a “straight arm plank.”

Step 2

Lift yourself in the air. Once you are in the proper position, lift your body up in the air with your toes on the ground, your back straight and your gaze looking slightly forward. Make sure to keep your abdominals contracted the whole time you do this.

Step 3

Place your hands next to each other. The plank position is the high point of your close-grip pushups. Once you are there, bring your hands together so your thumbs and index fingers form a triangle.

Step 4

Perform your pushups. Lower your body down until your chest is 3 to 4 inches above your hands. Push yourself back up until your arms are straight.

Step 5

Perform your required repetitions as quickly as possible.

Close Grip Pushups

Child Pose to Cobras

Step 1

Kneel and sit on your feet with your heels pointing outward. Your knees should be separated, about the width of your hips.

Step 2:

Place your forehead on the floor, and then swing your arms forward.

Step 3:

Rest your forehead on the floor, and then bring your arms around and to your sides, palms facing upward.

Step 4

Extend forward until lying on your stomach.

Step 5:

Lie on your belly, while your head rests on your lower arms.

Step 6

Raise your forehead, look upwards and stretch your hands backwards. Let your weight rest on your chest.

Step 7

The head falls a little backwards towards your back and the backward movement proceeds from the neck and the chin. Move your belly further backward as if someone is pulling your arms. The weight is more and more shifted towards the belly and the lower back does the real work.

Step 8

If you cannot raise your chest any further, put your hands and arms next to your chest on the mat without losing the bend. Stretch your arms so that they stand perpendicular on the floor and at the same time turn your arms a little inward. Relax your lower back and bear your weight with your arms.

Step 9

The buttock muscles remain relaxed during the exercise. Move your chest further upward with every breath out. Do this in a relaxed way instead of using force. You can tilt your head back. The shoulders are broad in front and the shoulder blades remain low.

Step 10

Repeat for required number of repetitions.

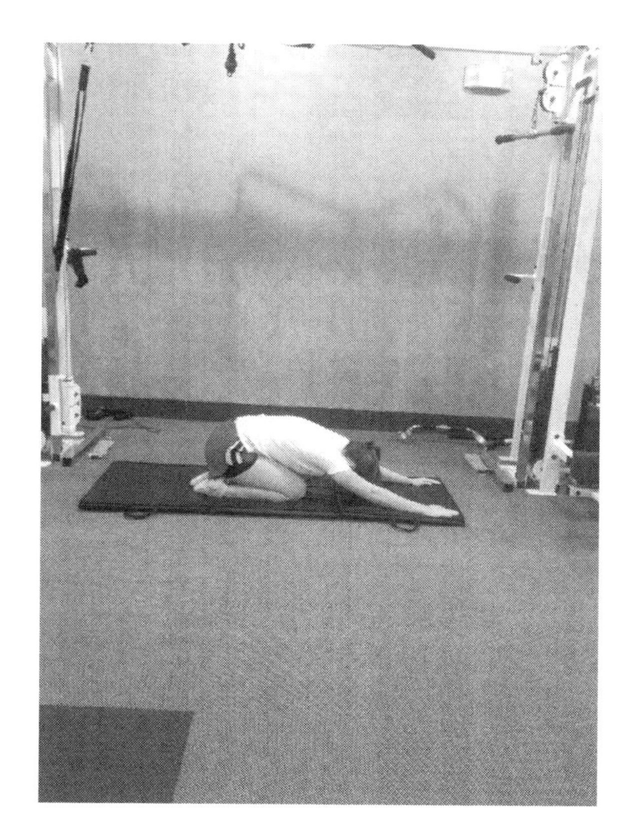

Child's Pose

Cobra Pose

Striders to Runner Pose

Step 1

Start in the plank position – or the push-up position – with your hands under your shoulders and your legs extended out.

Step 2

Lift one knee to your chest and keep your other leg extended straight out behind you with your toe on the floor and your heel lifted into the air.

Step 3

Rest your chest on your thigh and keep your head up with your eyes facing in front of you.

Step 4

Keep your knee over your ankle and extend your straightened arms to the ground, locking your elbows and putting the fingertips on the ground.

Step 5

Hold the pose, driving your back heel to the ground and your front thigh forward.

Step 6

Return to Plank

Step 7

Step your other leg forward

Step 8

Repeat for the required number of repetitions.

Striders to Runner Pose

Stride To Runner Pose Front

Striders To Runner's Pose Profile

Striders to Runner Pose with Twist

Step 1

Start in the plank position – or the push-up position – with your hands under your shoulders and your legs extended out.

Step 2

Lift one knee to your chest and keep your other leg extended straight out behind you with your toe on the floor and your heel lifted into the air.

Step 3

Rest your chest on your thigh and keep your head up with your eyes facing in front of you.

Step 4

Keep your knee over your ankle and extend your straightened arms to the ground, locking your elbows and putting the fingertips on the ground.

Step 5

Hold the pose, driving your back heel to the ground and your front thigh forward.

Step 6

Rotate from the waist as your inside arm is rotated towards the ceiling.

Step 7

Return to Plank

Step 8

Step your other leg forward

Step 9

Rotate from the waist as your inside arm is rotated towards the ceiling.

Step 10

Repeat for the required number of repetitions.

Plank Pose

Striders To Runner's Pose With Twist

Band Pull Apart

Step 1

Stand with feet shoulder width apart.

Step 2

Grasp a medium strength resistance band with both hands in front of your body.

Step 3

Raise your arms to shoulder height, extended in front of your body.

Step 4

Keep your arms parallel with the ground; pull the band apart until your arms form a t.

Step 5

Slowly return to the start position of step 3.

Step 6

Repeat for the required number of repetitions.

Band Pull Apart Start

Band Pull Apart Horizontal

Band Pull Aparts Diagonal

Band Pull Apart with Dislocations

Step 1

Stand with feet shoulder width apart.

Step 2

Grasp a medium strength resistance band with both hands in front of your body.

Step 3

Raise your arms to shoulder height, extended in front of your body.

Step 4

Keep your arms parallel with the ground; pull the band apart until your arms form a t.

Step 5

Slowly raise your arms overhead as your rotate your arms backwards as far as possible

Step 6

Slowly return to the start position of step 3.

Step 7

Repeat for the required number of repetitions.

Starting Position

Step2

Step 3

Finish

Backward Roll into Plough Back into Straddle

Step 1

Stand with feet shoulder width apart, squat down until your hands touch the floor.

Step 2

Use momentum roll backwards towards the floor.

Step 3

As you roll, extend your legs outward, until your reach plough pose.

Step 4

Exhale and bend from the hip joints to lower your toes to the floor above and beyond your head. As much as possible, keep your torso perpendicular to the floor and your legs fully extended.

Step 5

With your toes on the floor, lift your top thighs and tailbone toward the ceiling and draw your inner groins deep into the pelvis. Imagine that your torso is hanging from the height of your groins. Continue to draw your chin away from your sternum and soften your throat.

Step 6

You can continue to press your hands against the back torso, pushing the back up toward the ceiling as you press the backs of the upper arms down, onto your support. Or you can release your hands away from your back and stretch the arms out behind you on the floor, opposite the legs. Press the arms actively down on the support as you lift the thighs toward the ceiling.

Step 7

Forcefully roll forward while bring your legs towards front

Step 8

As you roll forward. Extend your legs out to the sides as wide as possible.

Step 9

Land in a straddle stretch hinge forward at the waist; reach as far forward as possible.

Step 10

Immediately begin to roll back into plough pose.

Step 11

This is a rapid and rhythmic shift that is repeated for the required number of repetitions.

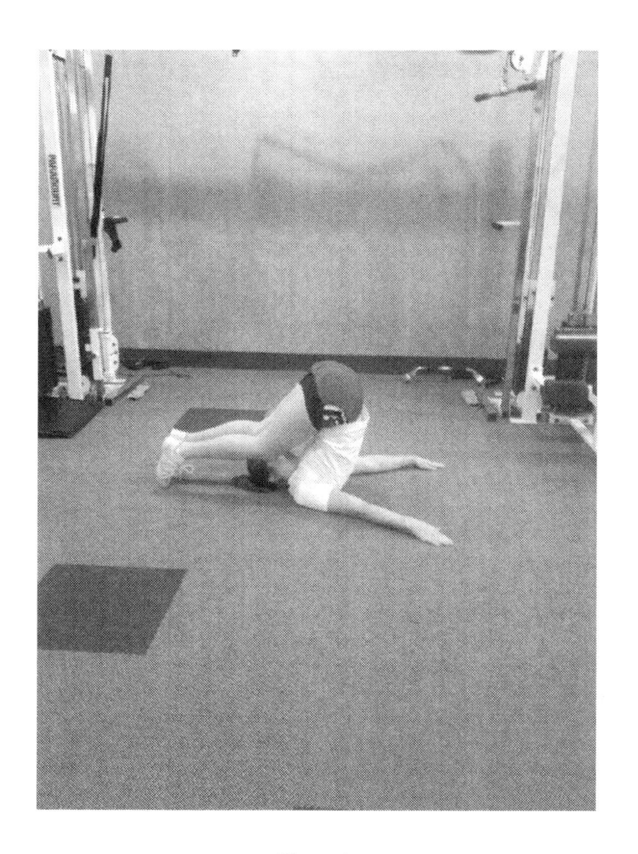

Plough

Straddle

Backward Roll into Plough Back into Glute Stretch

Step 1

Stand with feet shoulder width apart, squat down until your hands touch the floor.

Step 2

Use momentum roll backwards towards the floor.

Step 3

As you roll, extend your legs outward, until your reach plough pose.

Step 4

Exhale and bend from the hip joints to lower your toes to the floor above and beyond your head. As much as possible, keep your torso perpendicular to the floor and your legs fully extended.

Step 5

With your toes on the floor, lift your top thighs and tailbone toward the ceiling and draw your inner groins deep into the pelvis. Imagine that your torso is hanging from the height of your groins. Continue to draw your chin away from your sternum and soften your throat.

Step 6

You can continue to press your hands against the back torso, pushing the back up toward the ceiling as you press the backs of the upper arms down, onto your support. Or you can release your hands away from your back and stretch the arms out behind you on the floor, opposite the legs. Press the arms actively down on the support as you lift the thighs toward the ceiling.

Step 7

Forcefully roll forward while bring your legs towards front

Step 8

Slide the right knee forward toward your right hand. Angle your right knee at two o'clock.

Step 9

At the same time slide your left leg back as far as your hips will allow.

Step 10

Keep your hips square to the floor. If your hips are not square, there will be unnecessary force on your back, and you won't be able to open the hips to their fullest.

Step 11

If you're not feeling a deep stretch in your right glute, slide the right foot forward–little by little–toward your left hand. With practice, bring your foot parallel with the front edge of your mat

Step 12

Your right thigh should have an external rotation, and your left thigh should have a slight internal rotation. This keeps pressure off the knee cap.

Step 13 Depending on how you feel; you will be upright on your hands while sinking the hips forward and down. Level two will rest on their forearms, and level three will rest the chest on the floor with the arms fully extended in front of you.

Step 14

Immediately begin to roll back into plough pose.

Step 15

Repeat steps 2 through 14 for your other leg.

Step 11

This is a rapid and rhythmic shift that is repeated for the required number of repetitions.

Plough Pose

Glute Stretch

Glute Stretch with Forward Hinge

Backward Roll into Plough Back into Seated Hamstring

Step 1

Stand with feet shoulder width apart, squat down until your hands touch the floor.

Step 2

Use momentum roll backwards towards the floor.

Step 3

As you roll, extend your legs outward, until your reach plough pose.

Step 4

Exhale and bend from the hip joints to lower your toes to the floor above and beyond your head. As much as possible, keep your torso perpendicular to the floor and your legs fully extended.

Step 5

With your toes on the floor, lift your top thighs and tailbone toward the ceiling and draw your inner groins deep into the pelvis. Imagine that your torso is hanging from the height of your groins. Continue to draw your chin away from your sternum and soften your throat.

Step 6

You can continue to press your hands against the back torso, pushing the back up toward the ceiling as you press the backs of the upper arms down, onto your support. Or you can release your hands away from your back and stretch the arms out behind you on the floor, opposite the legs. Press the arms actively down on the support as you lift the thighs toward the ceiling.

Step 7

Forcefully roll forward while bring your legs towards front

Step 8

As you roll forward. Extend your legs out to the sides as wide as possible.

Step 9

Land with both legs together and extended to the front. Hinge forward at the waist, reach as far forward as possible.

Step 10

Immediately begin to roll back into plough pose.

Step 11

This is a rapid and rhythmic shift that is repeated for the required number of repetitions.

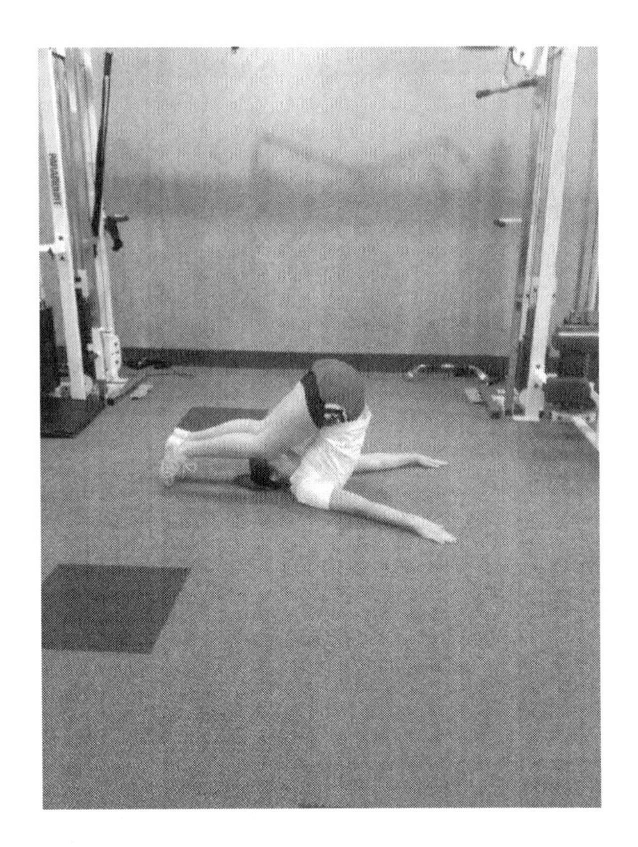

Plough Pose

Seated Hamstring

Deep Squat to Forward Lunge

Step 1

Stand with feet about shoulder width apart.

Step 2

Squat down with your butt back, your weight on your heels and your lower back in a neutral position.

Step 3

Push your hips back, keep your back straight, chest up and get your butt down below your knees. Keep your weight mostly on your heels. Once your reach the bottom of the movement, squeeze your gluts and push off of your heels to get into the standing position.

Step 4

Step forward with your right leg.

Step 5

Bend your knees until they are both approximately 90 degrees. Keep most of your weight on your front heel without letting your knee go too far past your toes. Also, keep your kneecap in line with your 2nd toe at all times during this exercise.

Step 6

Push back up to standing to complete one rep.

Step 7

Perform another squat.

Step 8

Step forward with your left leg. Perform a lunge.

Step 9

Continue to alternate legs until the required number of repetitions has been completed.

Start

Squat

Forward Lunge

Cossacks Squats/Lunge

Step 1

Take a wide plie stance with your toes pointing outward.

Step 2

Slowly squat down and slow shift your weight to your right side.

Step 3

Make sure your foot stays down on the side you have shifted your weight and that your knee tracks over your toes on this side.

Step 4

Your left leg should be straight, toes pointed to the sky and the heel remains on the floor.

Step 5

Slowly shift your weight to your left leg, until your right leg is straight, toes pointed and your heel on the floor.

Step 6

Repeat until the required number of repetitions has been completed.

Lunge Left

Transition

Lunge Right

Standing Glute Stretch

Step 1

Stand with your feet shoulder width apart.

Step 2

Lift your left leg, bringing your knee toward your chest.

Step 3

Wrap your arms around your left leg, and draw it tightly against your body.

Step 4

Lower your left leg and repeat the above steps with your right leg.

Step 5

Alternate legs until the required number of repetitions has been completed.

Standing Glute Stretch

Cradle Walks

Step 1

Stand with your feet shoulder width apart.

Step 2

Lift your left leg, bringing your knee toward your chest.

Step 3

Grab your left legs with both hands, rotate you're your hip up and out. Attempt to get your left foot parallel to the ground.

Step 4

Lower your left leg and repeat the above steps with your right leg.

Step 5

Alternate legs until the required number of repetitions has been completed.

Standing Cradle Walk

Strength Training for Competitive Cheerleading

Strength Training for Competitive Cheerleading

Competitive cheerleading is a dynamic sport that requires powerful, repeated muscle contractions. Functional cheer conditioning must include strength training instead of static, isometric training.

The shortening and lengthening of the muscle fibers during training is important because Cheerleading requires these muscle contractions in every stunt and body movement. Typically, cheerleaders use eccentric contractions to decelerate and control or stabilize the body. For example, eccentric contractions occur in your thigh muscles as your finish your back tuck. Concentric contractions occur in the hamstrings as you accelerate upward to start your back tuck.

Athletes can perform isotonic exercise with body weight, free weights, such as dumbbells or barbells, medicine balls, kettle bells, sand bags, rubber tubing, and weight machines. Although there is no one best form of isotonic exercise for the cheerleader each form has its advantages and disadvantages. For example, body weight is always available, but you cannot easily change your body weight as you get stronger to provide greater resistance.

Using free weights is a cost effective form of training that requires great control during lifting because there is no guide path or movement track like a weight machine offers. Using free weights forces cheerleaders to stabilize the weight in all directions while moving it in the primary movement pattern. This works secondary muscle groups that stabilize the joints you are exercising, but requires greater skill and supervision due to less control. One additional benefit of many weight machines is their ability to vary the resistance during the exercise range of motion.

Another type of resistance commonly use is rubber tubing or rubber cords. This form of resistance is desirable because it is cost effective, easy to travel with, and potent because the further the stretch the cord the greater the resistance generated.

Whatever type of isotonic exercise you select, the important factor is movement. The joints move, the muscles lengthen and shorten, and this mimics the actions during stunting, tumbling, or chanting. Most exercises in this chapter are isotonic exercises for the cheerleader.

They use free weight, sandbags and kettle bells to provide you with a resistance program using whatever methods available to you.

Isokentic resistance training uses a constant velocity and changing amounts of resistance. It uses a highly technical and expensive machine that does not allow most athletes to use this form of resistance in their training. Isokentic machines are used extensively in rehabilitating injuries and in research, and they have given sports scientist important information regarding the strengths and weaknesses of the muscular system of the cheerleader.

Within each type of resistance for increasing strength there are two primary forms of exercise. These two forms are single joint and multiple joint exercises. In a single joint exercise the athlete is exercising one primary joint and muscle group. For example, a knee extension exercise involves movement only at the knee joint and works primarily the quadriceps (front of thigh) muscle. A multiple joint exercise is one that works many muscles and muscles groups and includes movement at several joints simultaneously. A squat is a multiple joint exercise that works the gluteus, quadriceps, hamstrings, calf muscles, and others, with movement occurring at the hip, knee and ankle joints.

Both types of exercise are beneficial to the cheerleader. Multiple joint exercises work more muscles and joints simultaneously and certainly are time efficient. Multiple joint exercises require great balance. Proper form and training are essential to achieve the optimum benefit and prevent injury. Single joint exercises are beneficial when one muscle group is weak and the player has a muscle imbalance requiring exercise for one muscle group.

This particular program will use a large number of compound exercises and multiple methods to boost performance.

The first method will be through the use of complexes. In this method you combine two or more exercises performed back to back using the same resistance. For example you may group together a bent over row, shoulder press, and a squat. You would do all the required repetitions of the bent over row, then move directly to the shoulder press, complete the required number and then move directly into the squat, all without ever putting down the weight. Usually you perform 5 to 10 repetitions of each drill. You then repeat this entire collection for the required number of sets.

Another method you will use is density training. Density training is an excellent match for the requirements of today's athletes. Density training is about performing more work in a given time period. It works like this, you pick five exercises each loaded with a weight you can perform about 10 to 12 repetitions. You then perform 8 reps of each drill until you perform all of them; you continue to move through the circuit until your time is up. For example, how many times can you complete a series of bent over rows, lunges, shoulder press, zercher squats and kettlebell swings in 15 minutes?

Another way to use the same principle is to see how quickly you can perform 5 rounds of 8 reps in each of the bent over row, lunge, shoulder press, zercher squats and kettle bell swings.

One method helps develop strength endurance the other help develop speed strength, both are key to maximizing your all star performance. The goal is to develop fitter athletes that can either perform your planned choreography more easily resulting in fewer errors. You may also use this method to develop athletes that are fit and strong enough to include more elements in the 2:30 seconds allowed in competition.

This program also uses a timed method of intervals with varying ratios of work to rest periods. An example would be 30 seconds of squats followed by 30 seconds of rest for 8 rounds. The goal here is to achieve the maximum number of repetitions during the work interval.

What follows are some example workouts:

Sandbag Training Drills Descriptions and Demonstrations

Sandbag Drills and Descriptions

One of the best tools to improve your cheerleading performance is to use sand bags in your training.

What makes sandbags so useful for strength training for cheerleading?

Below are some general benefits of sand bag training.

1. They are very easy to learn so varying fitness levels can pick-up the technique of specific drills quickly while minimizing frustration.
2. They are very easy to transport which makes them ideal for large groups.
3. You can easily vary a drill to make it more difficult for a more advanced athlete or easier for someone beginning without having to make significant changes to the weight.
4. They are unstable so you can achieve the goal of training stabilizer and core strength.
5. They are easily adaptable to training the entire body.
6. Flexibility issues are minimized as most people can perform classic lifts such as squats better with implements such as sandbags because of the positioning of the weight.
7. Sandbags are possibly one of the safest tools available as you can drop them without fear of damaging the implement or surrounding area. This can give your athletes increased confidence to attempt drills normally they would be hesitant in performing.
8. They are relatively inexpensive compared to many other forms of training equipment. This makes it much more reasonable to utilize for class formats.
9. You can train various strength qualities such as strength-speed, strength-endurance, as well as perform conditioning. Such benefits make them a great tool for young athlete training.

10. They are FUN!! You can often create team building games and you can build competitions that achieve all your fitness goals while making training much more fun for your athletes.
11. Sandbags also allow some unique variety of exercises that make it novel to your athletes and it's really fun when they throw them.

Now I would like to give some more specific benefits unique to cheer fitness.

Sandbags are great tools because of the unstable, cumbersome nature of the training. This is a great way to develop core strength, upper back strength and lower body strength to boost performance quickly. Lifting and catching the unstable load of a sand bag is a great compliment or supplement to training for cheer stunts. It will allow your bases to develop strength without risking the health and safety of your flyers. The lifting and catching of sandbags will help your flyers better able to absorb the forces of being tossed and caught. A single training aid and program will improve the performance of bases, flyers and tumblers.

Another benefit of sandbag training is it mimics the static holds required in cheer and dance. Drills with sand bags will cause maximum isometric contractions in your athlete's hands, arms, back, core and legs. This will reduce the chance of injury, allow your team to practice longer, harder and safer.

These drills are the foundation of a program that will develop muscular endurance and strength that will translate to your performance very quickly. While there are many programs that will make you bigger and stronger in the gym, training with the shifting load of a sand bag will carry over to your sport.

Sandbags are a great way to train to improve your athlete's performance fast.

What follows are demonstrations and descriptions of several sandbag drills along with four sample circuits for you to use during the week.

Sandbag Shouldering

Step 1

Stand over the bag in a straddle position.

Step 2

Squat down with your butt back, your weight on your heels and your lower back in a neutral position.

Step 3

Grab the bag with straight arms.

Step 4

Use your legs to drive upward explosively.

Step 5

Use your arms only at the end of the movement to guide the bag to your shoulder.

Step 6

Lower the bag back down to the floor while pushing your hips back.

Step 7

Repeat for the prescribed number of reps.

Start

Shouldering Finish

Sandbag Shouldering with Squat

Step 1

Stand over the bag in a straddle position.

Step 2

Squat down with your butt back, your weight on your heels and your lower back in a neutral position.

Step 3

Grab the bag with straight arms.

Step 4

Use your legs to drive upward explosively.

Step 5

Use your arms only at the end of the movement to guide the bag to your shoulder.

Step 6

Push your hips back, keep your back straight, chest up and get your butt down below your knees. Keep your weight mostly on your heels. Once your reach the bottom of the movement, squeeze your gluts and push off of your heels to get into the standing position.

Step 7 Lower the bag back down to the floor while pushing your hips back.

Step 8

Repeat for the prescribed number of reps. Alternate sides each rep.

Start

Shouldering

Shouldering With A Squat Profile

Sandbag Clean and Press

Step 1

With your feet shoulder width apart, position the sandbag about a foot in front of you.

Step 2

Grab the sandbag with both hands about hip width apart, bending your hips with a slight bend in your knees.

Step 3

Keep your back straight and your glutes tight throughout the duration of the exercise.

Step 4

Bend your knees and lift your chest while keeping your arms straight---your butt should be lower than your shoulders. Stand up quickly and lift the sandbag off the floor.

Step 5

As the sandbag reaches waist height, pull with your arms and bring it to your shoulders.

Step 6

Rotate your hands under and push your elbows forward to catch the sandbag on upturned hands.

Step 7

Bend your knees slightly and then push the sandbag overhead to arms' length.

Step 8

Lower the sandbag to your shoulders and then to the floor and perform another rep.

Sand Bag Clean

Sandbag Press

Sandbag Rotations

Step 1

Lift the sandbag all the way up with your left arm passing above your head, and place it on your back just below the shoulder area.

Step 2

You might notice that your body will make a slight bend to the right as you lift the sandbag.

Step 3

Lower the sandbag the same way you did in lifting it to your back.

Step 4

Lift it all over again, but this time to the other direction.

Step 5

As your right arm passes above your head, your torso then makes a slight bend to the left.

Step 6

Repeat for the required number of repetitions.

Rotation Left

Rotation Right

Sandbag Bent Over Rows

Step 1

With your feet shoulder width apart, position the sandbag about a foot in front of you.

Step 2

Grab the sandbag with both hands about hip width apart, bending your hips with a slight bend in your knees. Your grip maybe close, wide, neutral or in a bear hug grip.

Step 3

Grab the bag and come to a full standing position.

Step 4

Bend at the hips and stick the butt back with a slight bend in the knees.

Step 5

Keep a strong arch to the low back and the chest sticking outwards; pull the sandbag towards the lower part of the chest.

Step 6

Make sure to squeeze the shoulder blades back and drive the elbows upwards.

Sandbag Row Start

Sandbag Row Finish

Sandbag Clean

Step 1

With your feet shoulder width apart, position the sandbag about a foot in front of you.

Step 2

Grab the sandbag with both hands about hip width apart, bending your hips with a slight bend in your knees.

Step 3

Keep your back straight and your glutes tight throughout the duration of the exercise.

Step 4

Bend your knees and lift your chest while keeping your arms straight---your butt should be lower than your shoulders. Stand up quickly and lift the sandbag off the floor.

Step 5

As the sandbag reaches waist height, pull with your arms and bring it to your shoulders.

Step 6

Rotate your hands under and push your elbows forward to catch the sandbag on upturned hands.

Step 7

Lower the sandbag to your shoulders and then to the floor and perform another rep.

Start

Clean

Sandbag Zercher Squats

Step 1

With your feet shoulder width apart, position the sandbag about a foot in front of you.

Step 2

Grab the sandbag with both hands about hip width apart, bending your hips with a slight bend in your knees.

Step 3

Keep your back straight and your glutes tight throughout the duration of the exercise.

Step 4

Bend your knees and lift your chest while keeping your arms straight---your butt should be lower than your shoulders. Stand up quickly and lift the sandbag off the floor.

Step 5

As the sandbag reaches waist height, pull with your arms and bring it to your shoulders.

Step 6

Hold the bag in the crooks of your arms.

Step 7

Keep the chest tall slowly squat downwards by placing your bodyweight on your heels.

Step 8

Try to squat deep in between your legs keeping the elbows up and don't let the chest sink down.

Step 9

Drive through your heels to come back to the start position.

Step 10

Repeat for the required number of repetitions.

Zercher Hold

Zecher Squat

Sandbag Zercher Reverse Lunges

Step 1

With your feet shoulder width apart, position the sandbag about a foot in front of you.

Step 2

Grab the sandbag with both hands about hip width apart, bending your hips with a slight bend in your knees.

Step 3

Keep your back straight and your glutes tight throughout the duration of the exercise.

Step 4

Bend your knees and lift your chest while keeping your arms straight---your butt should be lower than your shoulders. Stand up quickly and lift the sandbag off the floor.

Step 5

As the sandbag reaches waist height, pull with your arms and bring it to your shoulders.

Step 6

Hold the bag in the crooks of your arms.

Step 7

To begin, your feet should be shoulder width apart, torso erect with arms hanging straight at your sides, palms facing in.

Step 8

Take a slow, controlled lunge (or large step) backwards with your left foot.

Step 9

Lower your hips so that your right thigh (front leg) becomes parallel to the floor. At this point your right knee should be positioned directly over your ankle and your right foot should be pointing straight ahead.

Step 10

Your left knee should be bent at a 90-degree angle and pointing toward the floor. Your left heel should be lifted.

Step 11

After reaching the bottom of the movement (when your left knee is almost touching the floor), pause for a moment, or a breath, then push with your left, or back foot to move almost straighten both legs (photo on the left). Keep both feet on the ground – you are not returning to the starting position, just raising your pelvis up a bit and almost straightening your knees.

Step 12

This completes one, now bend your knees and lower your pelvis down to complete another.

Step 13

Return to the starting position (standing with both feet underneath your pelvis); now repeat the movement on the other side, stepping back with the right foot

Step 14

Repeat for the required number of repetitions.

Zercher Hold

Zercher Hold Reverse Lunge Profile

Zercher Hold Reverse Lunge Front View

Sandbag Power Clean and Zercher Squat.

Step 1

With your feet shoulder width apart, position the sandbag about a foot in front of you.

Step 2

Grab the sandbag with both hands about hip width apart, bending your hips with a slight bend in your knees.

Step 3

Keep your back straight and your glutes tight throughout the duration of the exercise.

Step 4

Bend your knees and lift your chest while keeping your arms straight---your butt should be lower than your shoulders. Stand up quickly and lift the sandbag off the floor.

Step 5

As the sandbag reaches waist height, pull with your arms and bring it to your shoulders.

Step 6

Rotate your hands under and push your elbows forward to catch the sandbag on upturned hands.

Step 7

Keep the chest tall slowly squat downwards by placing your bodyweight on your heels.

Step 8

Try to squat deep in between your legs keeping the elbows up and don't let the chest sink down.

Step 9

Drive through your heels to come back to the start position.

Step 10

Lower the sandbag to your shoulders and then to the floor and perform another rep.

Step 11

Repeat for the required number of repetitions.

Start

Clean

Zercher Squat

Sandbag Zercher Good Mornings

Step 1

With your feet shoulder width apart, position the sandbag about a foot in front of you.

Step 2

Grab the sandbag with both hands about hip width apart, bending your hips with a slight bend in your knees.

Step 3

Keep your back straight and your glutes tight throughout the duration of the exercise.

Step 4

Bend your knees and lift your chest while keeping your arms straight---your butt should be lower than your shoulders. Stand up quickly and lift the sandbag off the floor.

Step 5

As the sandbag reaches waist height, pull with your arms and bring it to your shoulders.

Step 6

Hold the bag in the crooks of your arms.

Step 7

Keeping your legs straight bend forward from your waist until a good stretch is felt or

Until you have reached a comfortable range of motion.

Step 8 Straighten yourself back up to a standing position and repeat for the desired

Repetitions.

Start

Finish

Sandbag Pull Through

Step 1

Stand straight with your legs shoulder width apart. Straddle the sandbag.

Step 2

Lean forward at your waist slightly and bend your knees so as to go into a semi-squat. Keep your back arched and head facing forward steadily.

Step 3

Grab the sandbag with both hands

Step 4

Let you arms hang loosely and raise the weight to shoulder height right hand and inhale. Then, swing the weight with in between the legs towards the back of you while exhaling. Move the sand bag using power thrusts from the hip, thigh, and lower back muscles.

Step 5

Repeat for the required number of repetitions.

Sandbag Pull Through Start

Sandbag Pull Through Top

Kettlebell Training Drills Descriptions and Demonstrations

Kettlebell Drills and Descriptions

You can improve your cheerleading performance by following this highly effective strength and conditioning program designed to boost explosive power, enhance endurance, improve strength, reduce the chance of injury, and improve overall performance in a minimum amount of time.

What is a Kettlebell?

A kettlebell basically is a cast iron ball with a handle on it. They have been used in Russia for centuries by their Olympic athletes and Military. They are small and come in various weights. They are a very versatile tool to add to your cheerleading conditioning program.

What Makes a Kettlebell Different?

The design makes the kettlebell different. When you hold a kettlebell, the weight is displaced differently. There is a constant pulling on you due to the center of mass being different. With dumbbells the weight is evenly distributed over your hand. When you hold a kettlebell, the weight is not distributed evenly, forcing you have to counter balance. This makes it a perfect training aid for developing the strength of your bases and flyers, given the unstable and shifting balance that occurs during a stunt.

The handle on the kettlebell makes the weight easier to hold for ballistic drills and also adds a pulling, due to momentum and gravity during drills. Your athletes have to actively counter with tension in the muscles of their body. This makes the drill harder, more effective and creates a very efficient and effective workout that mimics the demands stunting and tumbling place on the body.

Adding kettlebell training to your conditioning program will produce measurable results that will show in your athlete's performance quickly.

How to Hold a Kettlebell

There are numerous ways to hold a kettlebell, varying the grip allows you change the intensity of the drill you are performing. I will share the six grips I use most often with my cheer athletes

1. Standard hold.
2. Reverse grip
3. Two hand hold
4. Reverse two hand hold(Bottoms Up)
5. Flat Palm hold/Reverse Palm Hold
6. Ball grip

Standard Hold

Begin with the kettlebell on the floor in front of you. The kettlebell should be outside of the hand you will be using for the drill. Slide your fingers through the handle, palms facing towards you. When you close your hand the bottom of kettlebell is next to your forearm.

Reverse Grip

This grip is the same as the standard hold with the exception you begin with the kettlebell inside your forearm.

Two Hand Hold

Begin with the kettlebell on the floor in front of you in the center of your body. Grasp the handle with both of your hands. You may place your hands directly on top or the handle or grab along the side post portion of the handles. The bottom of the kettlebell will be pointing downward.

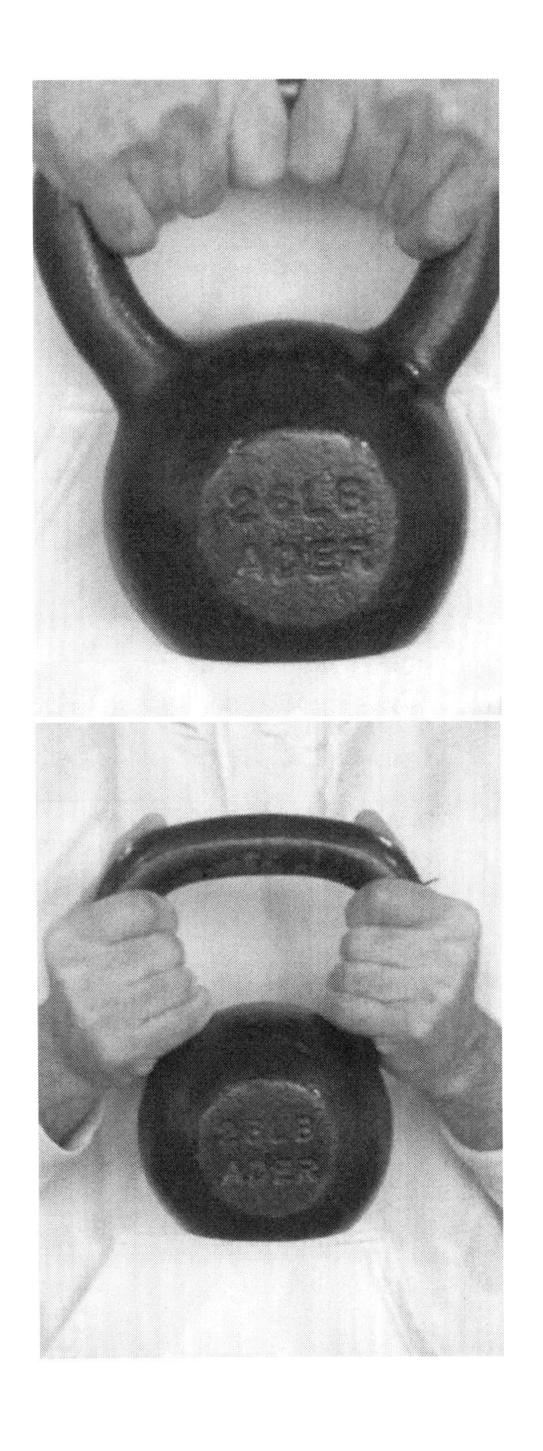

Reverse Two Hand Hold

Begin with the kettlebell on the floor in front of you in the center of your body. Grasp the handle with both of your hands. You may place your hands directly on top or the handle or grab along the side post portion of the handles. The bottom of the kettlebell will be pointing upward. This grip is often called the bottoms up grip.

Palm Hold

With this grip you place the bottom of the kettlebell in the bottom of your hand. Your fingers should point away from your face and level with your palm. The handle can point up, down or sideways. You may reverse this grip by place the bell in the palm of your hand with your fingers facing you.

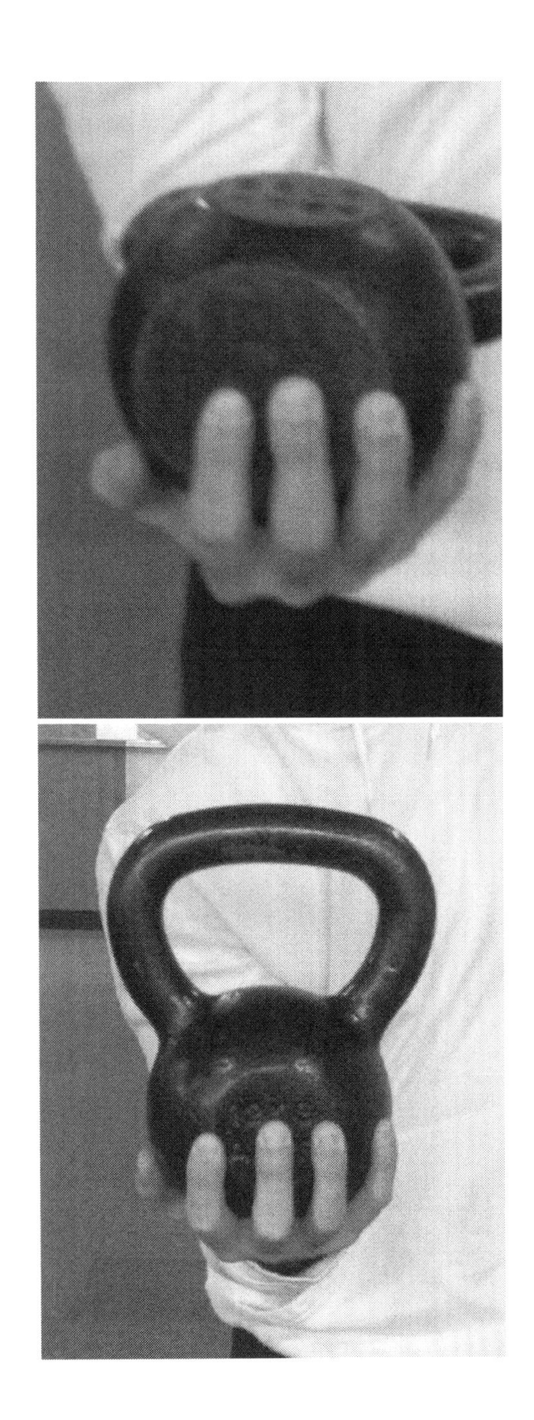

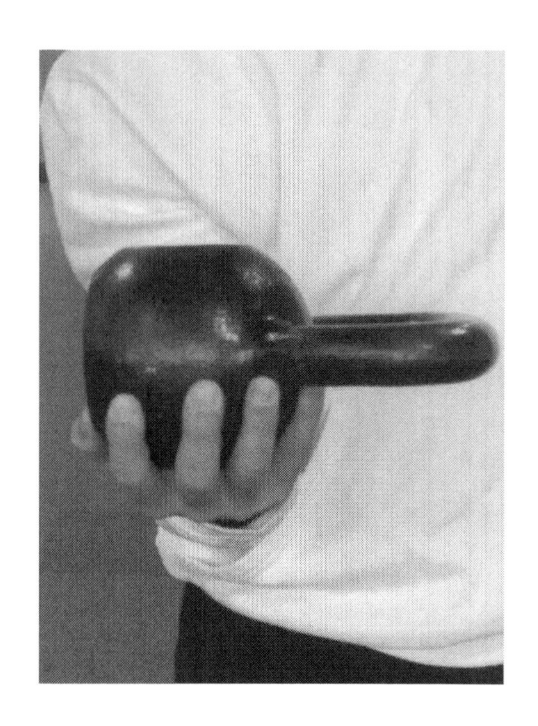

Ball Grip

Begin with the kettlebell on the floor in front of you in the center of your body. Grab the kettlebell with both hands around the bottom (ball portion). Your fingers are open, hands press hard into the side of the ball. The handle may point up or down.

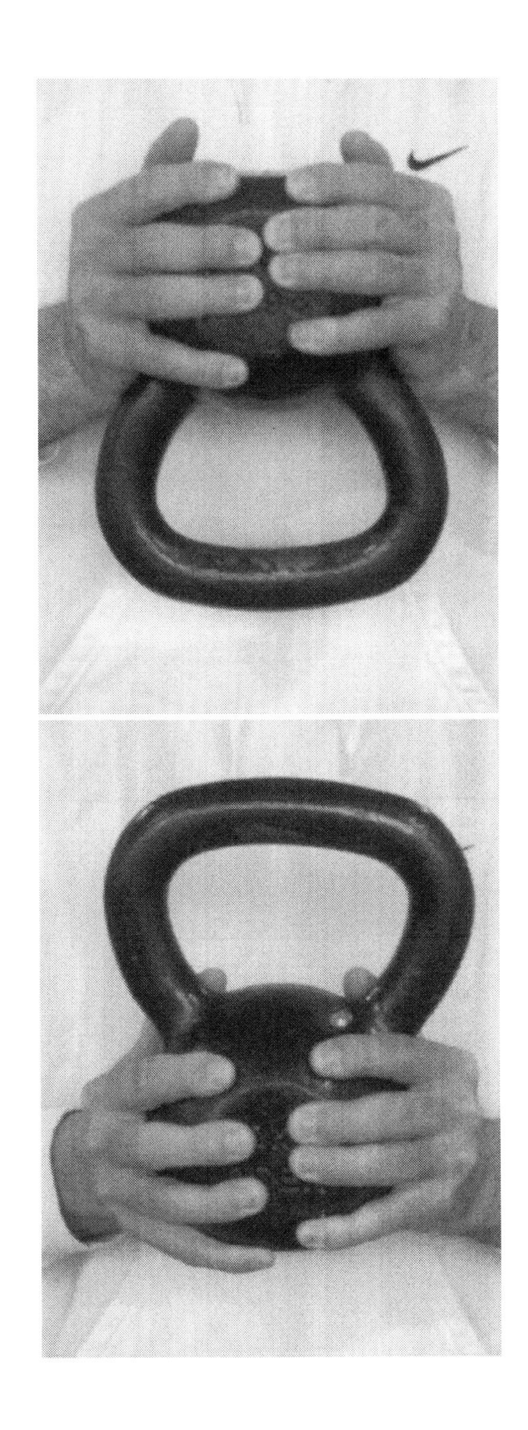

Kettlebell Swing

Step 1

Stand straight with your legs shoulder width apart.

Step 2

Lean forward at your waist slightly and bend your knees so as to go into a semi-squat. Keep your back arched and head facing forward steadily.

Step 3

Try a light kettlebell first. Let you arms hang loosely and raise the weight to shoulder height and inhale. Then, swing the weight with in between the legs towards the back of you while exhaling. Move the kettlebell using power thrusts from the hip, thigh, and lower back muscles.
Powerful hip snap on every rep are musts.

Step 4

With heavier weights, inhale on the swing between your legs and exhale when you raise it above your head.

Start of Swing

Kettlebell Switch

Step 1

Stand straight with your legs shoulder width apart.

Step 2

Lean forward at your waist slightly and bend your knees so as to go into a semi-squat. Keep your back arched and head facing forward steadily.

Step 3

Try a light kettlebell first. Let you arms hang loosely and raise the weight to shoulder height right hand and inhale. Then, swing the weight with in between the legs towards the back of you while exhaling. Move the kettlebell using power thrusts from the hip, thigh, and lower back muscles. A powerful hip snap on every rep are must.

Step 4

Perform 30 seconds of kettlebell swings with a minute pause between each set of repetitions. With heavier weights, inhale on the swing between your legs and exhale when you raise it above your head.

Step 5

Grip a light kettlebell with your right hand.

Step 6

Straighten your arm, lock your elbow, and then swing the kettlebell from your right arm to shoulder height. At the apex of the movement, release your right hand and grab the kettlebell with your left hand. Repeat this for one minute. Rest for 30 seconds then move to your next drill. Power this movement from you hip muscles.

Start

The Kettlebell Clean

Step 1

With your feet shoulder-width apart, position the kettlebell about a foot in front of you.

Step 2

Grab the kettlebell, bending your hips with a slight bend in your knees.

Step 3

Keep your back straight and your glutes tight throughout the duration of the exercise.

Step 4

Pick up the kettlebell and swing between your legs, then swing the kettlebell forward to about chest level, using a hip-snapping motion.

Step 5

Keep your upper arm against your side and use a pulling up motion as if starting a lawn mower.

Step 6

Immediately use an uppercut motion, having the kettlebell end up between your forearm and biceps.

Start

Clean

The Clean and Press

Step 1

Stand over the kettlebell with you feet placed slightly wider than shoulder width apart. Make sure the kettlebell is centered between your legs.

Step 2

Squat down slowly as you keep your upper back straight and a "C" curve in your lower back (lumbar spine). Grab the handle of the weight with one hand and allow your other arm to rest towards your side in a neutral position.

Step 3

Stand up in the motion of a dead lift, being sure to keep your back straight. Swing the weight up towards your shoulder and allow it to turn so the ball of the weight swings around your hand and comes to rest on the top of your forearm. Bend your elbow completely, ending with your knuckles next to your outer chest and shoulder. As you clean the kettlebell, dip into the swing so your body lowers in order to catch the kettlebell in the up position.

Step 4

Straighten up into a standing position. Dip down again and push back up with your glutes, hamstrings and thighs. Press the kettlebell up to the sky as you push up. Get the weight to a fully raised position with your elbow locked. Keep it there for 1 second.

Step 5

Lower the kettlebell back to the up position that you started the press from. Dip down as you lower the weight so you're in a lowered position when you catch the weight by your shoulder. Then, stand up straight.

Step 6

Lower the weight to the floor, again paying attention so that your back remains straight with an inward curve in your lower back.

Start

Clean

Press

The Squat

Step 1

Begin by lifting the kettlebell into the standard rack position, common in many kettlebell training exercises. Place the kettlebell just a few inches in front of your feet. Spread your legs so that they are a bit further than shoulder width apart and squat down over the weight.

Step 2

Keep your back straight, your abdominals strong and your shoulders down and back. Your chest should lift up and out throughout the exercise and your gaze should be kept forward.

Step 3

Grasp the handle of the kettlebell and lift slightly. Swing the weight back through your legs to gain a bit of momentum and stand up straight on the uplift. As you lift the kettlebell to your shoulder, bring your elbow in tight to your body and the weight should naturally roll over your wrist to rest on your forearm in the rack position.

Step 4

Hold your non-working arm slightly out to the side to maintain your balance and bend at the knees into a squat position. With the kettlebell in rack position, lower and lift before gently releasing the weight to the ground.

Step 5

Repeat the kettlebell squat training exercise on the opposite side.

Squat Start

Squat Front View

Squat Profile View

The High Pull

Step 1

Use the kettlebell high pull either as an exercise in itself, or as a transition to begin other exercises. While performing your workout, it is important to remember that the center of your body's power is in the hips and legs. Lift the weight not just with your arms, but with your legs and center.

Step 2

Begin with your feet about shoulder width apart, resting a kettlebell between your legs with the handle horizontal to your body. Squat down and grip the kettlebell so that your knuckles face away from you. Keep your spine straight as you squat, lowing your body with your legs and only leaning forward with the hips if absolutely necessary. There should be no curve in your spine.

Step 3

Push into your feet as you engage your abdominal muscles and lift your body up, bringing the kettlebell with you. Lift the kettlebell until it is at about shoulder level, bending the elbow slightly. At this point you can either move the weight into position for a variety of other exercises within your workout routine, or repeat the high pull.

Step 4

Repeat the high pull by allowing the kettlebell to fall as you squat once again. This time, allow the kettlebell to swing between your legs and then lift once again. Always complete the same number of repetitions on both sides of your body.

Start

High Pull

The Snatch

Step 1

Stand with your legs shoulder width apart and position the kettlebell about a foot in front of you.

Step 2

Grab the kettlebell, bending your hips with a slight bend in your knees.

Step 3

Keep your back straight and your glutes tight throughout the entire exercise.

Step 4

Pick up the kettlebell swing it between your legs.

Step 5

Using a hip-snapping motion thrust the kettlebell forward and at the same time, pulling up as if starting a lawn mower.

Step 6

When the kettlebell reaches its peak above your head with your arm almost fully extended, punch up through the kettlebell letting it rest on your forearm.

Step 7

From here, let the kettlebell drop out in front of you making sure it does not jerk your shoulder at any point. Make sure the kettlebell is neither too far out in front or too close to you during the drop.

Step 8

Swing the kettlebell between your legs and repeat.

Start

Pull into Snatch

Snatch Position

Kettlebell Exercise Tables

Exercise			
	Time	Repetitions	Notes
Kettlebell Swings Right Hand			
Kettlebell Swings Left Hand			
Kettlebell Switches Right Hand			
Kettlebell Switches Left Hand			
Kettlebell Cleans Right Hand			
Kettlebell Cleans Left Hand			
Kettlebell Clean and Press Right Hand			
Kettlebell Clean and Press Left hand			
Kettlebell Squat Right Hand			
Kettlebell Squat Left Hand			
Kettlebell High Pull Right Hand			
Kettlebell High Pull Left Hand			
Kettlebell Snatch Right Hand			
Kettlebell Snatch Left Hand			

Training Methods and Sample Programs

Beginner Sandbag Complexes

Beginner Sandbag Complex	Weeks 1-2 3 sets 6 reps 2 Minute Rest Between rounds	Weeks 3-4 3 Sets 7 Reps 2 Minute Rest Between Rounds	Weeks 5-6 3 Sets 8 Reps 90 Seconds Rest Between Rounds
	Weight	Weight	Weight
Shouldering	Set 1 Set 2 Set 3	Set 1 Set 2 Set 3	Set 1 Set 2 Set 3
Clean and Press	Set 1 Set 2 Set 3	Set 1 Set 2 Set 3	Set 1 Set 2 Set 3
Bent Over Row	Set 1 Set 2 Set 3	Set 1 Set 2 Set 3	Set 1 Set 2 Set 3

Beginner Sandbag Complex	Weeks 7-8 3 sets 9 reps 90 Seconds Rest Between rounds	Weeks 9-10 3 Sets 10 Reps 75 Second Between Rounds	Weeks 11-12 3 Sets 8 Reps 60 Seconds Rest Between Rounds
	Weight	Weight	Weight
Shouldering	Set 1 Set 2 Set 3	Set 1 Set 2 Set 3	Set 1 Set 2 Set 3
Clean and Press	Set 1 Set 2 Set 3	Set 1 Set 2 Set 3	Set 1 Set 2 Set 3
Bent Over Row	Set 1 Set 2 Set 3	Set 1 Set 2 Set 3	Set 1 Set 2 Set 3

Beginner Kettlebell Complexes

Beginner Kettlebell Complex	Weeks 1-2 3 sets 6 reps 2 Minute Rest between rounds	Weeks 3-4 3 Sets 7 Reps 2 Minute Rest Between Rounds	Weeks 5-6 3 Sets 8 Reps 90 Seconds Rest Between Rounds
	Weight	Weight	Weight
Right Arm Swing	Set 1 Set 2 Set 3	Set 1 Set 2 Set 3	Set 1 Set 2 Set 3
Left Arm Swing	Set 1 Set 2 Set 3	Set 1 Set 2 Set 3	Set 1 Set 2 Set 3
Right Arm Snatch	Set 1 Set 2 Set 3	Set 1 Set 2 Set 3	Set 1 Set 2 Set 3
Left Arm Snatch	Set 1 Set 2 Set 3	Set 1 Set 2 Set 3	Set 1 Set 2 Set 3

Beginner Kettlebell Complex	Weeks 7-8 3 sets 9 reps 90 Seconds Rest between rounds	Weeks 9-10 3 Sets 10 Reps 75 Second Between Rounds	Weeks 11-12 3 Sets 8 Reps 60 Seconds Rest Between Rounds
	Weight	Weight	Weight
Right Arm Swing	Set 1 Set 2 Set 3	Set 1 Set 2 Set 3	Set 1 Set 2 Set 3
Left Arm Swing	Set 1 Set 2 Set 3	Set 1 Set 2 Set 3	Set 1 Set 2 Set 3
Right Arm Snatch	Set 1 Set 2 Set 3	Set 1 Set 2 Set 3	Set 1 Set 2 Set 3
Left Arm Snatch	Set 1 Set 2 Set 3	Set 1 Set 2 Set 3	Set 1 Set 2 Set 3

Intermediate Sandbag Complexes

Intermediate Sandbag Complex	Weeks 1-2 3 sets 6 reps 2 Minute Rest between rounds	Weeks 3-4 3 Sets 7 Reps 2 Minute Rest Between Rounds	Weeks 5-6 3 Sets 8 Reps 90 Seconds Rest Between Rounds
	Weight	Weight	Weight
Shouldering	Set 1 Set 2 Set 3	Set 1 Set 2 Set 3	Set 1 Set 2 Set 3
Power Clean with Zercher Squat	Set 1 Set 2 Set 3	Set 1 Set 2 Set 3	Set 1 Set 2 Set 3
Zercher Good Mornings	Set 1 Set 2 Set 3	Set 1 Set 2 Set 3	Set 1 Set 2 Set 3
Bent Over Row Underhand Grip	Set 1 Set 2 Set 3	Set 1 Set 2 Set 3	Set 1 Set 2 Set 3

Intermediate Sandbag Complex	Weeks 7-8 3 sets 9 reps 90 Seconds Rest between rounds	Weeks 9-10 3 Sets 10 Reps 75 Second Between Rounds	Weeks 11-12 3 Sets 8 Reps 60 Seconds Rest Between Rounds
	Weight	Weight	Weight
Shouldering	Set 1 Set 2 Set 3	Set 1 Set 2 Set 3	Set 1 Set 2 Set 3
Power Clean with Zercher Squat	Set 1 Set 2 Set 3	Set 1 Set 2 Set 3	Set 1 Set 2 Set 3
Zercher Good Mornings	Set 1 Set 2 Set 3	Set 1 Set 2 Set 3	Set 1 Set 2 Set 3
Bent Over Row Underhand Grip	Set 1 Set 2 Set 3	Set 1 Set 2 Set 3	Set 1 Set 2 Set 3

Intermediate Kettlebell Complexes

Intermediate Kettlebell Complex	Weeks 1-2 3 sets 6 reps 2 Minute Rest between rounds	Weeks 3-4 3 Sets 7 Reps 2 Minute Rest Between Rounds	Weeks 5-6 3 Sets 8 Reps 90 Seconds Rest Between Rounds
	Weights	Weights	Weights
Swings Right Hand	Set 1 Set 2 Set 3	Set 1 Set 2 Set 3	Set 1 Set 2 Set 3
Swings Left Hand	Set 1 Set 2 Set 3	Set 1 Set 2 Set 3	Set 1 Set 2 Set 3
Switches Right Hand	Set 1 Set 2 Set 3	Set 1 Set 2 Set 3	Set 1 Set 2 Set 3
Switches Left Hand	Set 1 Set 2 Set 3	Set 1 Set 2 Set 3	Set 1 Set 2 Set 3
Clean and Press Right Hand	Set 1 Set 2 Set 3	Set 1 Set 2 Set 3	Set 1 Set 2 Set 3
Clean and Press Left Hand	Set 1 Set 2 Set 3	Set 1 Set 2 Set 3	Set 1 Set 2 Set 3

Intermediate Kettlebell Complex	Weeks 7-8 3 sets 9 reps 90 Seconds Rest between rounds	Weeks 9-10 3 Sets 10 Reps 75 Second Between Rounds	Weeks 11-12 3 Sets 8 Reps 60 Seconds Rest Between Rounds
	Weights	Weights	Weights
Swings Right Hand	Set 1 Set 2 Set 3	Set 1 Set 2 Set 3	Set 1 Set 2 Set 3
Swings Left Hand	Set 1 Set 2 Set 3	Set 1 Set 2 Set 3	Set 1 Set 2 Set 3
Switches Right Hand	Set 1 Set 2 Set 3	Set 1 Set 2 Set 3	Set 1 Set 2 Set 3
Switches Left Hand	Set 1 Set 2 Set 3	Set 1 Set 2 Set 3	Set 1 Set 2 Set 3
Clean and Press Right Hand	Set 1 Set 2 Set 3	Set 1 Set 2 Set 3	Set 1 Set 2 Set 3
Clean and Press Left Hand	Set 1 Set 2 Set 3	Set 1 Set 2 Set 3	Set 1 Set 2 Set 3

Advanced Sandbag Complexes

Advanced Sandbag Complex	Weeks 1-2 3 sets 6 reps 2 Minute Rest Between rounds	Weeks 3-4 3 Sets 7 Reps 2 Minute Rest Between Rounds	Weeks 5-6 3 Sets 8 Reps 90 Seconds Rest Between Rounds
	Weight	Weight	Weight
Shouldering	Set 1 Set 2 Set 3	Set 1 Set 2 Set 3	Set 1 Set 2 Set 3
Shouldering with Squat	Set 1 Set 2 Set 3	Set 1 Set 2 Set 3	Set 1 Set 2 Set 3
Clean and Press	Set 1 Set 2 Set 3	Set 1 Set 2 Set 3	Set 1 Set 2 Set 3
Bent Over Row	Set 1 Set 2 Set 3	Set 1 Set 2 Set 3	Set 1 Set 2 Set 3
Power Clean with Zercher Squat	Set 1 Set 2 Set 3	Set 1 Set 2 Set 3	Set 1 Set 2 Set 3
Zercher Good Mornings	Set 1 Set 2 Set 3	Set 1 Set 2 Set 3	Set 1 Set 2 Set 3
Pull Through	Set 1 Set 2 Set 3	Set 1 Set 2 Set 3	Set 1 Set 2 Set 3

Advanced Sandbag Complex	Weeks 7-8 3 sets 9 reps 90 Seconds Rest between rounds	Weeks 9-10 3 Sets 10 Reps 75 Second Between Rounds	Weeks 11-12 3 Sets 8 Reps 60 Seconds Rest Between Rounds
	Weight	Weight	Weight
Shouldering	Set 1 Set 2 Set 3	Set 1 Set 2 Set 3	Set 1 Set 2 Set 3
Shouldering with Squat	Set 1 Set 2 Set 3	Set 1 Set 2 Set 3	Set 1 Set 2 Set 3
Clean and Press	Set 1 Set 2 Set 3	Set 1 Set 2 Set 3	Set 1 Set 2 Set 3
Bent Over Row	Set 1 Set 2 Set 3	Set 1 Set 2 Set 3	Set 1 Set 2 Set 3
Power Clean with Zercher Squat	Set 1 Set 2 Set 3	Set 1 Set 2 Set 3	Set 1 Set 2 Set 3
Zercher Good Mornings	Set 1 Set 2 Set 3	Set 1 Set 2 Set 3	Set 1 Set 2 Set 3
Pull Through	Set 1 Set 2 Set 3	Set 1 Set 2 Set 3	Set 1 Set 2 Set 3

Advanced Kettlebell Complexes

Advanced Kettlebell Complex	Weeks 1-2 3 sets 6 reps 2 Minute Rest between rounds	Weeks 3-4 3 Sets 7 Reps 2 Minute Rest Between Rounds	Weeks 5-6 3 Sets 8 Reps 90 Seconds Rest Between Rounds
Exercise	Weight	Weight	Weight
Swings Right Hand	Set 1 Set 2 Set 3	Set 1 Set 2 Set 3	Set 1 Set 2 Set 3
Swings Left Hand	Set 1 Set 2 Set 3	Set 1 Set 2 Set 3	Set 1 Set 2 Set 3
Switches Right Hand	Set 1 Set 2 Set 3	Set 1 Set 2 Set 3	Set 1 Set 2 Set 3
Switches Left Hand	Set 1 Set 2 Set 3	Set 1 Set 2 Set 3	Set 1 Set 2 Set 3
Cleans Right Hand	Set 1 Set 2 Set 3	Set 1 Set 2 Set 3	Set 1 Set 2 Set 3
Cleans Left Hand	Set 1 Set 2 Set 3	Set 1 Set 2 Set 3	Set 1 Set 2 Set 3
Clean and Press Right Hand	Set 1 Set 2 Set 3	Set 1 Set 2 Set 3	Set 1 Set 2 Set 3
Clean and Press Left Hand	Set 1 Set 2 Set 3	Set 1 Set 2 Set 3	Set 1 Set 2 Set 3
Squat Right Hand	Set 1 Set 2 Set 3	Set 1 Set 2 Set 3	Set 1 Set 2 Set 3
Squat Left Hand	Set 1 Set 2 Set 3	Set 1 Set 2 Set 3	Set 1 Set 2 Set 3
High Pull Right Hand	Set 1 Set 2 Set 3	Set 1 Set 2 Set 3	Set 1 Set 2 Set 3
High Pull Left Hand	Set 1 Set 2 Set 3	Set 1 Set 2 Set 3	Set 1 Set 2 Set 3
Snatch Right Hand	Set 1 Set 2 Set 3	Set 1 Set 2 Set 3	Set 1 Set 2 Set 3
Snatch Left Hand	Set 1 Set 2 Set 3	Set 1 Set 2 Set 3	Set 1 Set 2 Set 3

Advanced Kettlebell Complex	Weeks 7-8 3 sets 9 reps 90 Seconds Rest Between rounds	Weeks 9-10 3 Sets 10 Reps 75 Second Between Rounds	Weeks 11-12 3 Sets 8 Reps 60 Seconds Rest Between Rounds
Exercise	Weight	Weight	Weight
Swings Right Hand	Set 1 Set 2 Set 3	Set 1 Set 2 Set 3	Set 1 Set 2 Set 3
Swings Left Hand	Set 1 Set 2 Set 3	Set 1 Set 2 Set 3	Set 1 Set 2 Set 3
Switches Right Hand	Set 1 Set 2 Set 3	Set 1 Set 2 Set 3	Set 1 Set 2 Set 3
Switches Left Hand	Set 1 Set 2 Set 3	Set 1 Set 2 Set 3	Set 1 Set 2 Set 3
Cleans Right Hand	Set 1 Set 2 Set 3	Set 1 Set 2 Set 3	Set 1 Set 2 Set 3
Cleans Left Hand	Set 1 Set 2 Set 3	Set 1 Set 2 Set 3	Set 1 Set 2 Set 3
Clean and Press Right Hand	Set 1 Set 2 Set 3	Set 1 Set 2 Set 3	Set 1 Set 2 Set 3
Clean and Press Left Hand	Set 1 Set 2 Set 3	Set 1 Set 2 Set 3	Set 1 Set 2 Set 3
Squat Right Hand	Set 1 Set 2 Set 3	Set 1 Set 2 Set 3	Set 1 Set 2 Set 3
Squat Left Hand	Set 1 Set 2 Set 3	Set 1 Set 2 Set 3	Set 1 Set 2 Set 3
High Pull Right Hand	Set 1 Set 2 Set 3	Set 1 Set 2 Set 3	Set 1 Set 2 Set 3
High Pull Left Hand	Set 1 Set 2 Set 3	Set 1 Set 2 Set 3	Set 1 Set 2 Set 3
Snatch Right Hand	Set 1 Set 2 Set 3	Set 1 Set 2 Set 3	Set 1 Set 2 Set 3
Snatch Left Hand	Set 1 Set 2 Set 3	Set 1 Set 2 Set 3	Set 1 Set 2 Set 3

Density Training Samples and Logs

Density Training Day One

Drill	Weight Used	Time of Circuit	Sets Completed
Day 1			
Sandbag Shouldering			
Sandbag Shouldering with Squat			
Sandbag Clean and Press			
Sandbag Bent Over Row			

Density Training Day Two

Day Two	Weight Used	Time of Circuit	Sets Completed
Sandbag Shouldering			
Sandbag Power Clean + Zercher Squat			
Sandbag Zercher Good mornings			
Sandbag Bent Over Row Underhand Grip			

Density Training Day Three

Day Three	Weight Used	Time of Circuit	Sets Completed
Sandbag Shouldering			
Sandbag Zercher Reverse Lunges			
Sandbag Power Cleans			
Sandbag Bent Over Rows Bear Hug Grip			

Density Training Day Four

Day Four	Weight Used	Time of Circuit	Sets Completed
Sandbag Clean and Press			
Sandbag Zercher Squats			
Sandbag Pull Through			
Sandbag Bent Over Rows Close Grip			

####

I Can Help You Personally in Your Quest for Championships!

Many cheerleaders and teams (maybe yours) want to move ahead, but are uncertain of the right game plan, much less the right workouts.

I can help you.

I can consult with you, I can create game plans for you, I can help create training programs to use, and I can do a customized, personalized clinic for any number of people on your team. I can create and generate individual and team success.

Please contact my team of friendly, helpful people.

Alton Skinner

919-270-4658

Altonskinner.com

Altonskinner@gmail.com

Acknowledgments

Writing is always a collaborative effort. Without a reader, these are useless words written for the ego of the author. So thank you for taking the time to read this project.

I am grateful to all the athletes, coaches, doctors, trainers, tumbling instructors, choreographers, uniform designers, judges and cheer competition organizers that took time out of their busy schedule to answer my myriad of questions to help make this project a useful tool to help improve the sport of competitive cheerleading.

I'd also offer a big thank you to Libby Reiher for helping out at the photo shoot. This book would not be possible without her willingness to take time during the competition season to learn all the drills and model them effectively as only a cheerleader could.

Also, a massive thank you and lots of love to Laura, my wife, for her help as sounding board, editor, inspiration and for being my loudest cheerleader.

Alton Skinner

About the Author:

Alton Skinner, is a strength coach and athletic performance nutritionist. He has spent near two decades helping athletes across a wide variety of sports to achieve their athletic goals. His clients range from mixed martial artists, national champion college golfers and teams, national and regional champion junior tennis players and teams, multiple Ms. North Carolina and Ms. South Carolina pageant winners, Ms. United States winners, elite age-group endurance athletes, gymnasts, members of the North Carolina Ballet, Fortune 500 executives and national/state champion All Star and High School cheerleaders. He has consulted for members of the NFL, NHL, MLB, NASCAR, PGA and LPGA on subjects of nutrition, training, and gym design.

He is a martial artist, yoga/Pilates instructor and ultra marathon runner. Alton also is a cheer dad capable of a high level one cartwheel.

Support good causes- 10% of all author royalties are donated to support the awareness and fund special needs cheer programs and the Make-A-Wish Foundation.

Connect with Me Online:

Author Page: http://www.amazon.com/author/altonskinner
Website: http://www.altonskinner.com
Twitter: http://twitter.com/altonskinner
LinkedIn: http://www.linkedin.com/pub/alton-skinner/3a/714/503
Blog: http://winningworkoutsforcompetitivecheerleaders.wordpress.com
Google+profile:
https://plus.google.com/u/0/116082159178277141343/posts
Facebook: http://www.facebook.com/AltonSkinnerAthleticConsulting

Made in the USA
Charleston, SC
07 May 2012